HOMEMAKER'S RESPONSE TO INFLATION

HOMEMAKER'S RESPONSE TO INFLATION

JUDY HAMMERSMARK

haven books
Division of Logos International
Plainfield, N.J. 07060

All Scripture references are taken from the King James Version, unless otherwise noted TLB *(The Living Bible)*, RSV *(Revised Standard Version)*, or NEB *(The New English Bible)*.

Chapter 3, "Homemakers, Take a Bow" (originally "Happy at Home") and chapter 9, "You Can Be Beautiful" (originally "The Essence of Beauty") are reprinted with permission from *Virtue* magazine.

HOMEMAKER'S RESPONSE TO INFLATION
Copyright © 1980 by Logos International
All rights reserved
Printed in the United States of America
Library of Congress Catalog Number: 80-82774
International Standard Book Number: 0-88270-454-0
Logos International, Plainfield, New Jersey 07060

iv

For
LEE HOWRY
a great great-uncle

*"I am come that they might have life,
and that they might have it
more abundantly."*

(John 10:10)

Introduction

Let's face it. We live in difficult times. It often seems "the faster I go the behinder I get"—in the financial realm, in the realm of family living, in the aspect of physical and spiritual well-being.

The essence of this book is to discover ways to become better stewards of all the blessings that come to us in Christ. We can see victory with our money, our physical bodies, our family life, and our inner, spiritual character.

It is possible to live serenely, even in this twentieth century. Inflation, and all its attendant pressures, do not have to threaten the Christian homemaker.

This book was written to make life a little more peaceful, a little more fulfilling, for the women called by God to the challenging role of the Christian homemaker.

Contents

HOMEMAKER'S RESPONSE TO INFLATION

1

All that Glitters

During Harvard's 1978 commencement exercises, when the bearded Russian Aleksandr Solzhenitsyn leaped to his soapbox to announce in no uncertain terms that the American nation is headed for the dogs, many were affronted.

Americans wanted to know, "What does a Russian know about Americans, anyway?" We're not going to the dogs—we're just having a good time, we rationalize.

Tradition remains; the doomsayer will be discounted and disliked no matter how well-intentioned. (Remember Jeremiah? His detractors stuffed him down a well.) As addicts of Dr. Norman Vincent Peale's smiling philosophy, many Americans minimize the negative and accentuate the positive. We are skilled at making excuses for almost everything. So we have inflation—that indicates prosperity, doesn't it? Many teenagers smoke pot, consume cases of alcoholic beverages, and engage in sex on the sly, while defying every authority. Mere youthful experimentation, we rationalize.

We look at all the things we have and smile. Houses with three-car garages, water beds, expensive vacations—who could possibly want more?

And truly, we are a nation blessed. Our system of free enterprise has afforded incredible wealth. Our heritage is both rich and varied, incorporating all the knowledge of Rome, Athens, and Jerusalem, while utilizing all the newer innovations of capitalism, mass production, marketing, advertisement, and distribution.

In my middle-class home I know luxuries that even kings a century ago never dreamed of. My family enjoys all the conveniences of modern refrigeration, plumbing, and electricity. By the grace of Thomas Alva Edison my clothes are being laundered and dried and my dinner cooked even as I compose this on an electric typewriter.

Our society is probably the richest the world has ever known. American welfare recipients enjoy a higher standard of living than some of the more well-to-do in the Third World. Yet richness, luxury, materialism, as Solzhenitsyn solemnly prophesies, can be our undoing.

John Adams foresaw today's preoccupation with things material when he wrote to Thomas Jefferson in 1819, "Will you tell me how to prevent riches from producing luxury? Will you tell me how to prevent luxury from producing effeminacy, intoxication, extravagance, vice, and folly?" And Thoreau wrote from Walden Pond, "What is the nature of luxury which enervates and destroys nations?"

The riches of our external world can be both bait and snare if we permit them to overcome our sense of restraint and moderation. Says Malcolm Muggeridge, "Our civilization is sinking under the burden of its own wealth and the necessity to consume it . . ."

So many glittering things there are to entice us. Constantly I war with my acquisitive self. Going through the catalog I covet any number of items—a new spring outfit, a little blue hurricane lamp, a hutch for my kitchen. My list of must-haves goes on and on. Still, when I close the catalog and move outside into the bright world that God has made, I forget about acquiring things. Like Thoreau at Walden I become ever so briefly "monarch of all I survey."

Truly, our greatest gifts are very cheap! A

rosebud unfolds in the afternoon sunshine; a robin gathers twigs and string; clouds play tag across an azure sky. None of these can I possess, so I relax.

In the bloom of this materialistic twentieth century we are engaged in a battle between the carnal and the moral. Says Anne Morrow Lindbergh, "We throw ourselves indiscriminately into committees and causes; not knowing how to feed the spirit, we try to muffle its demands with distractions."

Things are not bad in themselves. Possessions delight us and enrich our lives. Materialism becomes crass only when we set things up as objects of worship. In our haste to get and spend many have fallen subject to material possessions. More and more energies must be spent keeping them up, making payments on time, adding to our collections. Thus, eventually love of God and family and service to others becomes secondary in our lives.

Freedom, we discover, is not always dependent on the form of government we live under. People can be enslaved without chains or prisons. Unrestrained buying on credit can make us slaves to those rectangular plastic cards.

One learns the true meaning of liberty

upon losing it, someone said. Through his long experience in Soviet concentration camps, Solzhenitsyn has become somewhat of an expert on lost liberty. Through insight gained in prison he has come to define freedom as an unflagging sense of responsibility, courage, and faith in God.

So many Americans today long for the kind of freedom that can only come from within. Driven by our human desire to gain and consume, many of us long for release from the strife within. We quest that island self which chooses to serve, to pray, to nourish our spirits as well as our senses.

I seek an understanding friend who will take my load, my acquisitiveness—for sometimes it seems more than I can bear alone. Who will share such a burden?

Christ will. He says, "Come to me, all who labor and are heavy laden, and I will give you rest. Take my yoke upon you, and learn from me; for I am gentle and lowly in heart, and you will find rest for your souls. For my yoke is easy, and my burden is light" (Matt. 11:28-30, RSV). In Christ we discover an answer to every human need. Through Scripture, through the indwelling of the Holy Spirit, we discover the middle path, a place where we can feel at home with both our human and our spiritual nature. Will I be separated from Him and His wisdom, driven by lust? Or will I instead be a person tempered by His infinite love, with passions firmly in reign?

2

Our Hurry-Scurry, Throwaway Society

The idyllic little stream flushes along, curving, winding, twining. In one momentous twist it culminates into leaps and hurdles over craggy boulders, then winds slowly down. At last it terminates in a serene mountain lake. Here weekenders congregate to romp and play, paying tribute to boats, motors, water skis, amid their festive picnics.

And what do we find in their wake?

Beside the lake, beneath the trees, fluttering and dancing in the breeze—litter!

A recent outing with a friend was marred when, after treating our kids to hamburgers and shakes, she stopped and swept our garbage from the back seat of her car onto the highway. Would my friend have dropped such refuse in her own front yard? Never. Yet she felt no compunction in making our state highway her own dumping ground.

In our parks, along the boulevards, beside the ambling, isolated brook, our aesthetic vision is blighted. Everywhere there is evidence of our throwaway society in the form of:

a broken beer bottle

scraps of worn out tires

a soiled Pamper

tin cans, plastic containers, paper cartons.

Our American way of haste constitutes a fall from grace, in my opinion. No longer do we have *time* to pick up our garbage. Our sense of social responsibility has dimmed. Legalism, as Solzhenitsyn points out, has blurred our national vision and sense of pride. Like those ancient Pharisees that Jesus dealt with, we are more concerned with the letter of the law then its spirit.

"I'm gonna be late" is muttered under the breath of the motorist who speeds to work. In a state of physical, mental, and spiritual exhaustion so many dash to make their payments on time. Fred and Janet, for example, at retirement age purchased a new boat, motor, and camper trailer. Now, instead of relaxing and enjoying their golden years together, they must keep on working. "We gotta make those payments," Janet says. In spite of ill health they both must punch the time clock. The ironic fact is that they have so little free time that they haven't had a chance to use their new boat, motor, or camper.

Thoreau said, "The cost of a thing is the amount of what I call life, which is required to be exchanged for it, immediately or in the long run." In light of these terms the price many of us pay for our possessions is very dear indeed.

Money and possessions have a way of distorting life's true values. What lasting joy can be found in things? Our ownership of anything is at best only temporary. Overnight our currency can fail; the stock market may plummet; power, money, and fortune can be pulled out from under us in the blink of an eye.

So many Americans live at such a clip they reserve no energy or time for the deepening of inner character. They skim life's surface; their faith at best is but an outward show. Deep-down feelings about spiritual matters are rare. Inner convictions scarce. The Holy Spirit goes begging. Then, through illness, financial disaster, or disgrace, many must take stock: Who am I? Where am I going?

At such a hectic pace many times feelings are submerged; vital, powerful emotions smothered. Intimacy, even between married couples, or children and their parents, is not fostered as it should be. No *time* is there to discuss differences, to defuse angry feelings, to give our emotions the attention they deserve. And in our haste there is no time with our Lord, no time for prayer or quiet moments of meditation.

No wonder today's America represents a hotbed of unresolved feeling and inner turmoil.

We take it for granted. Things wear out, break down, must be thrown away. Geared for obsoletion, it is easy to transfer this principle to our relationships with other human beings. Little time is spent mending, patching, repairing anything, and when human beings are involved, there is no time to make amends. To start anew is easier.

We are in the throes of a throwaway experiment. At Christmas time we purchase for our little girls Barbie dolls that can be traded in next year on a more improved model. Diapers, bibs, and Kleenex we flush away. Whole meals in the form of TV dinners can be purchased on throwaway trays. Fashion models parade in gowns, coats, pajamas— even wedding dresses—constructed out of paper.

Human life itself is reduced to a sliding

scale for convenience's sake. Schooled to think in terms of disposability, it is fairly easy to transfer our thinking from man-thing relationships to human ones. The little girl brought up to trade in her doll is psychically prepared for a world where a pregnancy may be disposed of should it prove untimely. Another flushable is marriage. If it becomes troubled, if the partners cannot immediately leap one of life's hurdles, then they rush to get a lawyer. Why waste one's time and energy trying to fix something up?

We suffer a surfeit of selection. No longer do our multiple choices include a moral aspect. Vital decisions are made without the complication of weighing right and wrong. Should I live with my boyfriend? The only consideration is convenience. Thinking in terms of good and evil is obsolete. The new religion preaches, If God is not dead, then he is certainly moribund.

Our no-deposit, no-return thinking has been extended to many of our children. In this liberated age it is logical for mother to drop baby off at the nursery on her way to her job. Success, we believe, depends on how well we subdue our maternal longings. In so many cases no longer does mothering involve a spiritual bond. Way down the list of modern priorities is the child's need for a stable home life.

Today's mad scramble for things, prestige, power distorts our perception of the really worthwhile. As Alfred Montapert writes in his book *The Supreme Philosophy of Man*, "Our quest for gold has robbed us of our sense of God."

Well-meaning parents buy off their children with things. After their son was arrested for drug dealing one mother cried, "But we gave him everything!" Everything but herself, her *time*, her love, her guidance. Truly our children need our presence more than our presents!

Oddly, looking back at my own childhood, one of the happiest periods I can recall is the time my family had the Asian flu. Both my parents worked during the great part of my growing up years. Usually whenever I had been ill, my mother's job robbed me of her caring presence. This time we were all forced by illness to stay at home for a few days. How I relished those few hours of togetherness! In spite of a soaring fever, I felt so very happy. Never before had I felt so loved and so secure.

"God made time, but man made haste," an

Irish proverb reads. Our American way of haste makes intimacy impossible. What has become of heart-to-heart chats? Without time for communication how do parents relay values to their children? No wonder the Christian faith has been given such short shrift. Parents do not have *time* to introduce to their children the person that is Jesus Christ.

Aleksandr Solzhenitsyn mournfully observes, "A total liberation has occurred from the moral heritage of Christian centuries with great reserves of mercy and sacrifice . . . .Man's sense of responsibility to God and society grows dimmer and dimmer."

For reflected in the national faith is the no-deposit, no-return turn of mind. The Christian religion has been replaced by a new faith based upon human feelings, humanism. This new religion teaches that man is the only solace of man. It has succeeded in writing struggle out of our children's existence, while at the same time morally disarming them. Separated from Christ and His Holy Spirit, we are in danger of producing a nation of super-educated men and women with the outstanding handicap of moral illiteracy.

In truth, there are values that cannot be

measured by a paycheck. While money represents a means to many ends, certain things it cannot purchase. Faith in God, for one. Courage and hope. We must learn anew that there is richness too in sharing—spending *time* with one's loved ones—in kindness, gentleness, health, peace of mind, laughter, love, and loveliness. Even if 50 million people testify that God is dead, it is still a foolish belief. For God's principles and laws go on functioning whether or not we abide by them.

Truly, today's values are constructed of paste and tissue paper!

3

Homemakers, Take a Bow

Values and principles. How are these best communicated to youngsters? Sociologists tell us that values are best transmitted via the family unit, through intimate, caring interaction between family members.

Imagine, if you can, that you are a cunning, diabolical genius bent on destroying the United States of America and the values it represents. Where would you begin?

You deduce that there is a means. The family, you understand, is the foundation for every civilization, and if you can foul it up, success will be yours! You know there is no way women can escape their supreme responsibility in civilized society without endangering civilization itself. So you begin your attack on the family with women. You spread the idea that women's work is meaningless, that tradition is nonsense, and that child care is not only tedious, but it counts for nothing. Your goal: to make women at home feel utterly and irrevocably worthless.

By design or by chance, today's American home is in trouble. Along with the falcon and the great blue whale, today's family has become an endangered species. Each day when I open our *Daily Times* there is evidence anew—a long listing of divorces.

Unfortunately, divorce as a solution to marital problems is not isolated to our small community. Since 1960, the number of divorces in the United States has doubled. Out of every two marriages now performed, one is ultimately bound for the divorce court.

What goes wrong? Could it be bleak reality versus starry-eyed illusion? After the honeymoon he cannot stand her failure to recap the toothpaste, and she did not bargain for his habit of loud belching after a meal.

Or is it deeper than that? Does it perhaps involve a breakdown of longstanding tradition, the recasting of basic life roles for men and for women? In some ways, too, could it involve superficial commitments, vows taken lightly—"We'll give it a try to see how it works"?

Perhaps too, could it involve the complication of two wage earners, plus the loss of the cohesive force of full-time women at home? According to a recent *Newsweek* article, "Only about one family in four now conforms to the stereotypical traditional image of breadwinning Dad, homemaking Mom and dependent children."

Truly a failed marriage becomes everybody's business. A marital breakdown affects more than just the two partners. It involves children, our nation, and our Lord. For when things go well with our families, life is worthwhile; but when the family falters, life somehow becomes less meaningful, in some cases becoming a desperate struggle to survive.

We can easily see that marriage is a child's concern. This is because the breakup of a youngster's home becomes etched into a young heart. Broken marriage is a nation's concern as well. As President James A. Garfield said, "The sanctity of marriage and the family make the cornerstone of our American society and civilization." And ultimately, aborted marriage becomes God's business. For through the sound working of family life we grow in love to become witnesses for His world.

In so many cases the husband today is no longer the head of the family, nor the wife its heart. There is a huge vacancy on the home front. To cope with inflation, to make ends meet, more and more American wives and mothers are working outside the home. We who do stay at home to care for our families are made to feel like social misfits. Sometimes I find myself wondering, "What is the value of my place in society?"

But in truth wives and mothers at home do make a vital contribution to our way of life. Let's examine briefly just how valuable a career at home can be. As a friend says, "Women at home provide the atmosphere under the nation's rooftops." And that atmosphere encompasses so many things, home-made bread, a hug for a husband after a hard day's work, a concerned ear for a teenager's problem. In short, a way of life that provides security and stability.

There was a time when mom took pride in her ability to stretch a dollar. Take left-overs, those odd bits stored in the refrigerator until whiskery with age. (Then and only then could they be thrown out.) With a "needy budget" incentive, moms could concoct hearty suppers out of those scraps.

Even today, an inflated dollar saved, an inflated dollar earned. With haircuts averaging $2.50, I estimate that by cutting my husband's and my son's hair during the past sixteen years, I have lopped off at least $1,000 from family expenses.

Recently Professor Kathryn E. Walker of Cornell University conducted a survey which shows that if the services women perform at home had to be purchased from outsiders they would cost $28,000 a year. Consider some of things we women do:

Laundry, mending, cooking, cleaning, canning. Even if we could hire someone to do these kind of jobs, I am certain they would want at least minimum wage.

Caring for, dressing, feeding, guiding, tutoring young children. Governesses and teachers are accustomed to earning $5.00 an hour or more.

Mediating quarrels, counseling. Professionals earn $5.00 an hour.

Taking care of sick children. Nurses earn $5.00 an hour.

Sending out birthday and get-well cards, setting up appointments. Secretaries earn $4.00 an hour.

This says nothing of time donated to our communities, our schools, and our churches.

Overlooked, too, is the possibility that through their managerial skills women at home can save as much money as an outside job would bring in. For example, my friend Elaine writes from Sioux City, Iowa, "We grossed about $11,500 last year." But through sound management, wise purchasing, and cautious use of credit they are living very well indeed.

My friends are buying their own home and a late model car. Elaine bakes her own bread, and rarely uses mixes of any kind. "I make my own scratch goodies," she says. "As for junk food—never! Not only is it too expensive, it's of no benefit to you at all. I give our daughter [Amy, who is two] fresh fruit and raw vegetables. She loves them! I stretch our meat out as much as possible. For instance, one chicken for two and sometimes three meals. First, fried chicken using drumsticks, thighs and breasts. Boil the rest for chicken and noodles or soup or casseroles. [If there's any fried chicken left in my house, I make fried rice.] In the summertime Ed does a lot of fishing, and in the fall hunting. We have lots of fish, rabbits, pheasants and ducks. We eat lots of casseroles too. That saves us the most dollars. In the summer we raise a garden, and we're learning to can different things. Next summer we hope to buy a freezer."

Elaine is a skilled seamstress, and her mother sews for her, too. "I go downtown and find a dress I like then go home and tell Mom about it. Usually for less than half the ready-made price Mom makes a nearly identical outfit." At other times Elaine buys clothing during sales, often saving half.

Through her husband's credit union they save money. A certain amount is deducted biweekly from his salary. Then it is forgotten about. From this fund, along with refunds from state and federal income taxes (he claims no deductions), they buy major items like furniture and appliances.

Unheralded, many others like Elaine make a vital contribution to the stability of our society. Take the young mother I saw in the store the other day. With a toddler in tow and one in the infant seat she represented a great many other young mothers. In my imagination I followed her home. How does she manage? I mean getting inside with all those groceries and babies is no mean feat. My back aches for her. Watch as she changes first one diaper, then another. As she sees to supper, she sets one of the children, a smiling boy with large hazel eyes, in the high chair. Singing and chanting Mother Goose rhymes she goes about her business. Now she peels the potatoes. Sets the table. Hubby arrives and they sit down to eat. Finally, after the dishes are done (her husband has gallantly bathed the babies), she relaxes for the first time in twelve hours.

Truly, it takes more endurance, more patience, more intelligence, more healthy emotion to keep a marriage alive and to raise a happy human being than to be a nuclear physicist, politician, or psychiatrist.

Where can you hire someone who would do all that mom does? What housekeeper thinks and rethinks before each purchase, weighing value against available cash? And in what department store do you purchase a commodity called love?

The more I look around, the more I am convinced—*women at home don't do that bad.* Even compared with double paycheck families, for expenses have a way of expanding to meet income.

Best-selling author Dr. James Dobson writes "Women today are in rebellion against God and tradition because society does not appreciate them enough. In a questionnaire I recently administered to young Christian mothers, their most common source of depression was clearly low self-esteem. On a broader scale, the painful devaluation provides the energy (and the anger) that powers the Women's Liberation Movement. If women felt genuinely respected in their roles as wives and mothers they would not need to abandon it for something better. If they felt equal with men in personal worth, they would not need to be equivalent with men in responsibility."

In truth the psychological as well as the material advantages to full-time homemaking can be monumental. In the area of child raising in particular. Just the other day a retired first-grade teacher from Thermopolis, Wyoming, said, "After forty-one years in the classroom, the one thing that stands out in my mind is that the most well-adjusted children came from homes where mom made a career of her home and family."

Christians have all the tools needed to build a happy home life. Biblical principles do work. The catch is, somebody must work them. Defined in the Scriptures are the roles to be assumed by husbands and wives. But somebody has to enact them. The Scriptures give abundant instructions, too, in how to properly bring up children. But somebody has to *be at home* to carry them out.

A woman at home—cook, psychologist, nutritionist, economist. Nurturer and comforter, sayer of prayers, "watcher of pots and rainstorms." The family that stays together needs that cohesive force of a woman at home.

It's high time our society give credit where credit is due. Women need to feel appreciated for their fundamental contributions to our way of life. As Dr. James Dobson says, "If only more of us could bask in the dignity and status of the job at home, then we could relay to our little girls the true wonder of being female."

4

By Bread Alone

Nothing can be more basic than our daily bread. Mass production of bread, however, often does not adequately fulfill our family's nutritional needs. For this reason more and more conscientious wives and mothers are baking their own. As I jot down these words from my kitchen table, a February snowstorm blankets the neighborhood. In the next room an open fire crackles quietly, warming the atmosphere. On the stove a cast iron kettle brims with simmering stew. In the oven six crusty loaves are nearly ready for the noonday meal. Who says that homemaking cannot be satisfying? Right now I feel like queen of the hearth, and I survey my principality with pride.

Still, all my days are not so satisfying as today. Sometimes I put off until the very last minute my meal planning. When they ask, "What's for dinner?", frequently I am stumped.

Too bad our kitchen activities have been

so downplayed. No longer is the kitchen the center of our lives with its breadbaking, canning, cookie making—all the eternal rites of meal making. Hamburger Helper, Betty Crocker, and TV dinners (while admittedly very helpful) have served to remove mom from the kitchen, and in the process from the center of our being.

Jutting from one wall in grandmother's kitchen was a majestic wood stove which radiated warmth throughout. In the kitchen a mother would quite literally bring up her brood in the way they should go as she attended to the never ending jobs of the kitchen. Today that majestic wood stove has been replaced by a smaller, more efficient gas jet, the fully electric range, or the superefficient microwave. No longer is mom needed to spend hours with pot roasts that cook at their own slow pace. In this hurry-up age we rely instead on automatic timers that start the meal while the lady of the house is still on the job. Pressure cookers deliver a stew fully done in fifteen minutes. Microwave ovens take the worry out of that perennial question, "What's for supper, mom?"

All are such marvelous innovations, yet something has gone out of our lives. Why is it on days like today I feel so essential and very needed? Why do I relate more warmly to all family members when I am preoccupied with breadmaking rather than bread-winning?

My friend Elaine Hampton writes of her cozy kitchen. "Though the stained glass of my kitchen be from little fingerprints . . .

> confession's here
> communion's here
> among the household hints.
> With cookie crumbs a trail of love
> please let my kitchen be
> a sharing place
> a learning place
> where you, Lord, walk with me."
> (*Here's What's Cooking* by Westside
> Community Club).

Even my kids sometimes pitch in and help with the process of breadbaking. Elevated to the counter by a spindle-backed chair, even the smallest youngster delights in the doughy process. Plastered with flour, my youngest literally pounces on the mass of dough, kneading and shaping (with my help) the lump into neat, even loaves.

Though time consuming, breadbaking is fairly easy. My friend Trudi, who gave me my current recipe and some valuable tips, feels that making bread is essential for her family's survival, since she lives in an isolated community where drifts sometimes reach the rooftops during the winter months. She mills her own flour in a grinder. Grinding flour the same day as baking aids in preserving vitamin content, she says.

Here's Trudi's recipe (which I double, making four loaves instead of two, or at times triple, making six).

Bone Meal Bread

1 pkg. dry yeast (or 1 tbsp.)
2½ cups hot water
½ cup brown sugar
1 tsp. salt
¼ cup shortening
5 cups whole-wheat flour and 3 cups white
1 scant tsp. bone meal (this optional, find it in a health store)

Here's the process. First soften the yeast in ½ cup of the water. Then combine the rest of the warm water, brown sugar, salt, and shortening. Next stir in the whole-wheat flour, 1 cup at a time, along with the bone meal. Mix well. Now stir in the softened yeast. Next add enough of the remaining flour to make a moderately stiff dough. Says Trudi, "The secret of good breadmaking is to learn just how much flour you need." Amount used depends on such variables as the temperature of the room, moisture in the air, moisture content of the flour, your elevation, and so on.

After adding enough flour so that the dough is no longer sticky, turn the mixture out onto a lightly floured board. Knead until smooth (about 12 minutes). Next let it rise until double in bulk. (To hasten the process place your bowl on a heating pad turned down to low.) Punch down the raised mass. Next shape it into loaves and place in greased loaf pans. Let rise again until double in bulk. The final step is to bake at 400 degrees for 30 minutes.

Baking bread is so vital a business because good bread is so fundamental to good health. The history behind bread (the staff of life) is quite interesting. Briefly let me give you a rundown.

According to writer Charles F. Vinson, in ancient Egypt, classical Greece and Rome, and in ancient Israel wheat was ground between millstones that crushed the grain. This primitive milling process produced a rich, whole-grain flour.

Common people at that time ate the whole grain; however, the more well-to-do could afford a white bread which was produced from a relatively white flour. In order to produce such flour whole wheat was sieved through papyrus, rushes, horsehair, or flax.

Thus whole wheat became associated with common people, and white flour became a sign of status for the upper classes.

Later, Western standards demanded "purer" foods. Many gullible people were fed the notion through mass advertising that because of its color, white flour was more desirable than its darker counterpart.

First to be discarded was the *bran*. The practice of removing this vital part of the wheat, science has shown, has resulted in, among other things, constipation and cancer of the colon. Grain's first three layers are contained in bran. Under the bran is *testa*, then *aleurone*, replete with protein and minerals. The *germ* is the grain's heart, and it contains a high percentage of protein, natural sugar, oil, vitamin E, vitamin B, and assorted trace minerals.

Although these parts of the grain account for only 12 percent of its weight, they contain nearly all the valuable nutrients of the grain. In our modern times these unaesthetic dark components are fed to animals, and the germ is sold in health stores. No wonder cattle and pigs thrive, while modern man is not doing so well!

A long shelf life is the main advantage of white flour. Our modern technology has provided means so that white flour will "stay fresh" almost indefinitely.

Here's how this "miracle" is accomplished. Unmilled grains are first treated with methyl bromide to keep the wheat from growing rancid in the bins. Then, after the flour is ground, it is aged. Chemicals are used to artificially age the flour. Agene, or nitrogen trichloride, was used until 1956, when it was found to produce convulsions in dogs and was suspected of causing eye problems in human beings. Chlorine dioxide is used today, and in one operation this chemical bleaches, ages, and preserves white flour.

Next the flour is conditioned for easier mixing. Calcium stearyl-2-lactylate is used to soften the flour and emulsify it.

Grocers keep bread on hand much longer than most customers suspect. Mass production bakeries, therefore, add still more chemicals to insure that their product will not go stale. Inhibitors, such as monoglycerides and diglycerides, diacetyltartaric acid, esters of monoglycerides and diglycerides, and so on, are added to the flour to maintain the appearance of freshness.

Still it is not ready for the batter. Mold and "rope" inhibitors and preservatives are added next. Not until all the chemicals are mixed in does the assembly line bread production begin.

Students of nutrition have sounded the warning against white bread for many years. For a double minus is delivered to those who continually ingest this product. Vital nutrients are first destroyed, only to be replaced by many highly questionable chemical additives.

On the other hand, proponents of the mass-marketed white bread claim there is "no real scientific basis" for the belief that whole-wheat flour is superior to the white.

Knowledge of vitamins and trace minerals weakens the argument favoring white flour. For during the process of milling, 40 percent of the chromium, 50 percent of the pantothenic acid, 30 percent of the choline, 86 percent of the manganese, 16 percent of the selenium, 78 percent of the zinc, 76 percent of the iron, 89 percent of the cobalt, 60 percent of the calcium, 78 percent of the sodium, 77 percent of the potassium, 85 percent of the magnesium, 71 percent of the phosphorus, 77 percent of the vitamin B-1, 67 percent of the folic acid, most of the vitamin A, 80 percent of the vitamin B-2, 81 percent of the B-3, 72 percent of the B-6, most of the vitamin D, and 86 percent of the vitamin E are removed.

To replace this, manufacturers "enrich" the white flour with three B vitamins—B-1, B-2, and B-3—and iron. This iron is in ferric form, which is not assimilated as readily as the kind found in natural wheat.

White bread, because of its lack of vital nutritional elements, can put a real crimp in the fueling and repair of the human body. Many modern ailments, such as heart attacks and diabetes, are related to man's preference for this food. Diabetes sufferers and heart attack victims are frequently deficient in chromium and vitamin E, which are richly supplied by whole-wheat flour.

Today's nutritional scientists have found chickens deprived of manganese do not grow, and become sterile. Likewise, a deficiency of zinc will produce dwarfs. The trace mineral cobalt, they know, is vital to developing blood cells. Calcium is essential to build healthy teeth and bones. Without sodium our bodies dry up or swell to the bursting point.

Nutritional scientists know, too, that magnesium strengthens the heart and muscles by activating exchanges of energy within the cells. Phosphorus mediates all the energy exchanges in our bodies, enabling us to move and walk and think.

Geneticists have discovered that RNA and DNA, the chemicals which pass along the genetic code, depend upon vitamins B-1 and B-12, and folic acid. Steroid hormones, they know, cannot be manufactured in the human system without pantothenic acid. Nerves cannot function without choline; vitamin A is vitally essential to normal reproduction, good eyesight, and healthy skin.

Nutritionists recognize vitamin B-2 as important to clear vision and the maintenance of soft tissues of the eyes, mouth, and tongue. Vitamin B-3, we know, is a safeguard against pellagra. Vitamin B-6 is essential in protein metabolism. Vitamin D prevents rickets, and vitamin E, among other things, performs a vital duty by carrying oxygen to the human cells.

These are powerful, vital tools of life, which are removed in the process of milling. When any are lacking the human body suffers. Each one of these elements is found in a balanced ratio in whole-wheat bread. All are missing to one degree or another in refined white flour.

"I don't save much by baking my own bread, so why bother?" my friend says. Even if I didn't save a penny, I would feel bread-baking is worthwhile, if only for its nutritional benefits. I do save, however. By buying flour supplies in bulk and on sale, I estimate I save about one-third of the store-bought price of whole-wheat bread.

Whole-wheat bread is available in almost every store, but in many cases it is even more laden with chemical softeners, agers, fresheners, and preservatives than its white counterpart.

Perhaps before you go into the bread business, you should review some of the common reasons for failure. If your bread turns out too porous, Trudi tells me this is caused by overrising, or possibly baking at too low a temperature. Dark and blistery? The result of underrising. Your dough won't rise, just sits there like a rock? Caused by too much kneading, or perhaps your yeast is outdated. (I keep mine in the freezer to insure freshness.) Streaked bread? Due to underkneading, or not kneading evenly. Unevenly done?

Check your pans. If they are old and dark, invest in new ones.

I feel magnificently competent after successful breadbaking. With my freezer overflowing with bread manufactured by my own hands, I feel good and thrifty and prosperous. To think, not long ago, I had given myself up as "hopeless" in the breadbaking department!

5

Recipes for Superb, Economical Soup

There is no spectacle on earth more appealing than that of a beautiful woman in the act of cooking dinner for someone she loves. (Thomas Wolfe)

"Don't be wasteful," mama always warned whenever my paring knife would cut too much meat with the peel. "A wasteful woman throws more out the back door than her husband can bring in the front door!" A friend tells me, "I marvel at my mother. She put four kids through college by sheer thrift and her uncanny ability to make a delicious meal out of almost nothing—scraps, leftovers, bones."

Could it be that those accumulated bits and pieces of food that we tend to think of as waste might finance a child's education? My own mother has a wonderful knack of turning the most basic foods into hunger-satisfying meals. Her way with a bone pinched many a penny to its Spartan limits. "Every recipe," she taught me, "is a theme which the ingenious cook might vary to accommodate the supplies one has on hand."

To this day she maintains that fancy cooks are expensive cooks. "Don't always be running to the store for a special ingredient. Use your creative powers instead. There's always something in your cupboard that will substitute."

Soups and stews were her specialty. At our house, as in Alice's Wonderland, there was "soup of the evening, beautiful soup." In this day of high-rise inflation, soup as a one-dish meal is coming back. In my own kitchen, for example, last night's Swiss steak provided a small, round bone as the starter for today's lunch. At 10:30 this morning I placed that bone and a quart of water in my pressure cooker. For one-half hour it simmered, and by 11:00, the thin stock was ready. Next I added one-half cup leftover corn, a handful of chopped celery, carrots, onions, and a quart of tomatoes, along with a handful of broken spaghetti. I let this covered brew simmer slowly. By noon our simple minestrone was ready for lunch.

"Sure beats canned," was my husband's comment during our shared noon meal. My sense of pride and independence overflowed.

For I had made *something delicious from scraps of leftovers*, a piece of bone I had been tempted to award the dog.

During the depression and the rationing of World War II, many women were forced to expand their creative powers in the kitchen. Leftovers and throwaway items were viewed with new interest. During these difficult times in our nation's history American homemakers found that they were utilizing many a latent talent, and were able to tuck away dimes and dollars due to greater thrift. By relying on inexpensive recipes she had brought with her from her Norwegian homeland, my mother-in-law saved money even during hard-up depression years.

Kumpa, one of her recipes, has become a family favorite. This one-dish meal is made from a ham hock, a beef shank, or salted mutton ribs.

Here's how to do it. Cover bones with water (about 3 quarts). Simmer for two to three hours. (To save energy use a pressure cooker, cutting time to ½ hour.) Next remove the meat from the fire and skim off excess fat by adding a tray of ice and a few cups of cold water. Next prepare the oatmeal dumplings.

Mix together in a large bowl:

1½ cup leftover mashed potatoes
3 eggs
2 cups oatmeal
3 medium raw potatoes ground or grated
Enough flour to hold this mixture together (about 1½ cups).

Bring skimmed broth to a boil. Next roll a dumpling into a ball about the size of a large walnut. Let it sit for about ten minutes to see if it holds together. If it falls apart add more flour and test again. When the dough holds together, form the rest of the batch into dumplings. Next simmer for one hour in the broth. Serve the finished dish along with meat from the bones and butter.

Leftover kumpa may be sliced and fried in butter as a good breakfast or lunch.

The late nutritionist Adelle Davis wrote in *Let's Cook It Right*, "If you want excellent soup go on a salvage drive." Save scraps of bone, chicken, ham, beef, pork, or turkey, she said. Cover the bones with water and a teaspoon of vinegar and salt to draw calcium from bones. For good nutrition, vegetables should be cooked as little as possible. Instead of boiling vegetables in the stock, add them to the seasoned broth a few minutes before serving. A delightful flavor can be had by very briefly frying vegetables in margarine or butter before adding them to the soup.

Likewise, meat should not be boiled. If it is it tends to become stringy and flavorless. Instead chop the meat and brown it in a pan. Add it like the vegetables, just before serving.

In order to stretch their grocery budgets a country mile, many homemakers keep soup stock in the freezer for hearty, hurry-up suppers. Unexpected company can be treated to French onion soup (onions sautéed in butter and added to broth, with a sprinkle of cheese on top). Other garnishes, such as chopped almonds, unpeeled chunks of apple, bacon bits, bread sticks, caraway, cumin, and dill seeds, lend a touch of elegance to otherwise plain soups.

"Rich Man's Stew" (so named for the pennies one can accumulate by serving it frequently) is a recipe devised by a friend, an avid gardener, in order to use her garden's abundance. (If you happen not to have one of the ingredients, then improvise!)

Here's how to concoct a rich man's stew. Crumble one bay leaf over 2 pounds of beef ribs in a large (6 quart) pot or pressure cooker. Simmer all morning. (If you use a pressure cooker cut the cooking time down to about 45 minutes.) Next add a cup of ice-cold water and a tray of ice to skim away fat. Next add 3 or 4 bouillon cubes, salt, and pepper. Cut into chunks four well-scrubbed potatoes, four carrots, and two sliced green peppers. Chop two stalks of celery, along with the leaves, one onion, and a clove of garlic. When the vegetables are tender add a dash of lemon juice, a teaspoon of Worcestershire sauce, and a pinch of allspice. Next thicken slightly with five tablespoons of pasted whole-wheat flour. A can of tomatoes can be added for an interesting variation.

Ultra-low-cost suppers can be made from seafood too. From fillet save the bony pieces. Sometimes I take a cut of halibut, cod, or salmon (whatever is on sale) and steam it in the pressure cooker until the bones are soft (about 25 minutes). Then remove from the heat and add ½ cup finely chopped celery and onion. To this add 1 cup milk and 4 tablespoons whole-wheat flour to thicken. Next cover and simmer without boiling. Add salt and pepper to taste, and garnish with paprika. Variations of this can be made with clams or oysters.

Shrunken dollars can be expanded! All we have to do is utilize our creative powers.

Actually mother's way with a bone can be almost as easy as opening a can, and certainly far more nourishing, with an important extra—the happy knowledge that I made it myself!

6

The Value of
Defensive Shopping

In grandmother's day thrift was a way of life. But consumerism had not yet been born. Grandmother kept a sharp eye out for shoddy goods and shady dealing. Take old Mr. Mallory, who ran the general store at the corner of Fifth and Pine. Granny was especially leery of him, for there were whisperings of sanded sugar, watered milk, graveled beans, and floor sweepings in the rice bin. Granny had to be on her toes to keep ahead of cheating tradesmen.

Today's marketplace, although modernized, is still fraught with danger. Economic advisor Sylvia Porter writes, "The American marketplace is a jungle." And if you don't know the rules of survival, you may very well perish. Unfortunately, many of us are not even faintly acquainted with the rules. Weaknesses and vulnerabilities accompany us whenever we shop. And unlike Thoreau (who had no taste for elegant frills), many of us find ourselves battling desire, appetites, and passions while attempting to stay within our means and to make intelligent, rational purchases.

As buyers we are besieged and battered. Not only from within, but on the outside too—by unscrupulous sellers, overeager advertisers, and zealous purveyors of easy credit. To be thrifty in this day and age is a real test and a challenge.

"Don't sell the steak, sell the sizzle" is the motto of the wizards of mass merchandising. As subjects of advertising campaigns we are all at times subconsciously influenced by Madison Avenue propaganda. Nabbed by the scruff of our emotions, we are literally carried away into irrational buying. In advertising seldom are real facts presented to be rationally assessed. Gimmicks are employed instead to dazzle potential purchasers. Do you, for example, buy the brand of toothpaste that guarantees glittering white enamel? Dentists testify that white teeth are very rare, that most teeth are not white at all, but off-white, nearer beige.

"Take the fear out of being close" renders many frantic for the *right* brand of deodorant. And more important, am I using the *correct* dish detergent? Will mother-in-law get a mirror image of herself in my china?

The Value of Defensive Shopping

Buyers must constantly beware! Take sales for instance. Many times sales do provide considerable savings, but at other times we discover that a bargain is not a bargain when it serves only to accumulate dust on the shelf. I have a long line of impulsive purchases, humiliating reminders of my flagging self-control. My breath waxes hot at the sign of a sale, any sale. I am a sucker for bargain items—slightly out of style shoes, beauty aids (which fail to beautify), wrinkle removers, soaps and creams. (Alarmingly, a pair of false eyelashes suffering from adhesive failure once slithered to my cuff like a hairy, long-legged spider during a dinner party.) Wigs—reds, blondes, frosted ones— a dozen or more, worn but once—take up space in my drawer. All of these bought on impulse, irrational purchases when defenses were down. I had to have them! Because they were on sale.

Sale compulsion is fairly universal. I remember in particular a neighbor from childhood. She was so crippled by arthritis that she could barely hobble around. Yet if she heard of a sale, she somehow scrambled to the store, hotfooting it to the bargain table. Truly, she's someone strange who doesn't love a bargain.

Still another dilemma presents itself whenever I do chance upon even a useful sale item. Now I must have riggings, trappings, accessories to go along with my new purchase. A new dress? Matching scarf, shoes, and a new handbag must be purchased for that all-together, coordinated look. Artificial needs have a way of gradually overtaking our natural ones for food and shelter.

Yes, we buyers must constantly be on the defensive. Upon buying a vacuum cleaner that stubbornly refuses to pick up lint, or a carpet that loses its shag, or a wash-and-wear shirt that does not wash or wear, do you long for Ralph Nader to rescue you? Perhaps what is needed is legislation that will make the marketplace safe for all us hurried and harried shoppers. Or is it? More and more laws cannot protect the shopper. Absolute legalism cannot remove the buyer's foolishness. More self-protection is needed.

We in America are privileged to live in a society where free enterprise reigns, where the buyer's market is a perpetual reality. Before we hand over our dollars we are wooed and won. Unlike the communist nations, where production is so curtailed that Soviet customers must endlessly wait in line, we in America are accustomed to prompt service, choices aplenty, and abundance in tastes, styles, and textures. Yet this blessing is a mixed one, fraught with hazard. And for this reason shoppers desperately need internalized principles of defensive shopping.

Better trained in earning than in spending, Americans become fair game for the huckstering that goes on in today's marketplace. Years ago girls learned thrift and homemaking while awaiting marriage. Today we teach our girls instead how to be secretaries, dental technicians, or nuclear physicists—while glossing over more practical courses in budgeting and home management. Husbands too acquire specific job skills, yet learn little about day-to-day survival. Essentials such as how to balance a checkbook or to shop for insurance or to read a contract are not taught in most schools today.

In today's market, plenteous choices provide us not only with variety but with pitfalls as well. Even astute shoppers are sometimes bamboozled. My husband and I would like to forget the camera we purchased from a door-to-door salesman for $400. Later we found the identical camera in a catalog for $90.

Instead of soap in a plain wrapper, today's shopper must decide between Zest, Lux, or Lifebuoy. Those in the market for a new sewing maching are confounded by ten or more basic models in the Singer line alone. Montgomery Ward stocks eight models of washing machines to select from. Unless we are experts in merchandising, we are often stymied. Which should I buy?

With so many products screaming for attention, with so many glittering gadgets, and with salespeople rapping at the door, many have fallen into the careless credit trap. As Dr. Ernst A. Dauer, a consumer credit authority, puts it, "The typical family no longer purchases only what it needs, it purchases what it would like to have, and its aspirations are continually expanding."

Without strong financial leadership, many families find bills drifting higher and higher. Lives are reduced to a nervous scramble from paycheck to paycheck, until the situation becomes so hopeless that drastic steps are resorted to—bankruptcy, divorce, even suicide.

Luckily my husband keeps a firm reign on our budget. "Free checking," he laboriously explains, "does not mean you can write checks without making deposits." In my case irrational buying is my expression of poor money management. Many girls, like myself, are trained for a debt mentality by generous moms who forgo things for themselves in order to dress their daughters in style. Jantzen, Koret, and Pendleton grace many a girl's closet. Later on young husbands must reeducate their wives' tastes or find themselves moonlighting.

"He who loves money shall never have enough," the Bible says. "The foolishness of thinking that wealth brings happiness! The more you have, the more you spend, right up to the limits of your income, so what is the advantage of wealth—except perhaps to watch it run through your fingers!" (Ecc. 5:10-11, TLB).

To become good stewards of God's bounty is a goal to strive for. Plan for the future. Making sense with one's dollars saves worry and confusion. Make money your servant, not your master. As trustee of a monthly paycheck, budget wisely. Set aside a certain amount for tithing, food, clothing, and savings. Then, whatever is left over can be expended on frills and fun.

Defensive shopping pays. The dollar stretches when I discipline myself to compare values, to shop around. Stores which offer a bargain in appliances do not always offer the same savings in food or clothing. Many businesses will take a cut in one department and make up for it in the next.

Scrutinize carefully before buying. Read labels to determine quality. In the grocery line, quality does not always equal costly. Pennies, even dollars, can be saved by purchasing top quality. For example, the bone, gristle, and fat obtained by buying the cheapest cuts of meat diminish the number of servings. When buying baked goods, sniffing and squeezing are not always reliable indications of freshness. Instead check the baking dates. Check dates on dairy goods, cottage cheese, and milk, too.

My husband and I have agreed. If we find a good savings, we will stock up. We buy beef by the half, cut and wrapped to be stored in the freezer. Orange juice is purchased by the case when on sale. Likewise canned vegetables and fruit. Last minute jogs to the stores are reduced when one keeps a full pantry.

Keep your defensive buyer's eye focused for reasonably priced substitutes. When lettuce soars to seventy cents a pound, buy cabbage instead and serve coleslaw. Be constantly aware of retailers' tricks. Items with the greatest markup are usually placed at the customer's eye level. Sugared cereals, candy, gums, and soft drinks are placed within a child's easy grasp for good reason.

Buy on the basis of intended use. Company coming? Ham or a special cut of beef is in order. For Monday night's supper, a slowly simmered chuck roast will serve the same purpose with equally nutritional value. Use quality carpet for high traffic areas of your home, but a cheaper grade will do in an area like a bedroom which is little traveled.

When buying furniture compare quality and price. Small-towners may find a trip to a city to compare values worth their while. Markup on furniture is very high, so it is often a good idea to offer the retailer a lower price.

Overshopping is caused by emotional shopping. Make it a rule never to shop when down in the dumps. In this condition you will be tempted to make unwise purchases in order to "do a little something special for myself." And by all means when hungry don't shop for groceries. I stockpiled over $100 worth recently, breaking the budget, because I was ravenous.

Be pleasant and courteous always, but do exercise your rights. If Sunday's fryer sniffs spoiled, then return it on Monday for a fresher substitute. Insist on repair or replacement for the vacuum cleaner that fails to function. When buying a new car, be certain you get all the checkups given under the seller's guarantee. Likewise, most clothing or furniture when flawed can be replaced or repaired under an implied or written guarantee. Dealers are almost always eager to keep your good will by making things right.

Write down everything you spend for a while. This discipline will make you aware of how your money goes, and it will remind you how fast little items add up. "Let the buyer beware" is ancient advice, but still it is true. Be cautious and be wary. Look the goods over. If you possibly can, take it home "on approval." One ounce of defensive shopping can be worth a whole gallon of noisy consumerism.

Fortunately, good money managers can be made as well as born. Pray about your shopping. Invite the Holy Spirit to go along with you on shopping trips. Praise the Lord—my normally acquisitive nature is in the process of transformation. Ever so gradually my impulsive purchases are decreasing. After balancing our checkbook of late, I have even seen a hint of a smile on my husband's face.

Next, we will explore ways and means to even greater savings by a search for financial freedom.

7

How to Manage
Your Money

Suppose (like a small gray mouse in a corner) you could go into your neighbors' home unobserved and listen to their conversation. What do you think you would hear? More often than not, if they were quarreling, their debate would involve money. Money, according to various surveys, is the chief cause of differences between husbands and wives. Even the most intimate marriages become battlegrounds when money worries take over.

Ken and Cora, for example, get along beautifully in all areas except the financial one. "If it weren't for money," he tells her, "our life together would be ideal." Moneywise, Ken and Cora, like many other couples, have not yet grown up. Where money is concerned they are still in the toddler stage. Ken and Cora use money like a sledgehammer to batter one another with emotionally.

Consider this scene, for instance. Cora, in a flurry of anger, greets Ken at the door, waving a letter in his face. "Here's another warning from Friendly Finance. I thought you paid them off."

"I was going to, but then you got that new pantsuit, so I decided that old Ken had something coming, too. Tell Friendly Finance to go fly a kite, Cora. We'll pay them when we get around to it. Now cheer up, dear. Look at this new camera outfit I got for the family— only $50 down and $10 a month—a real steal, Cora!"

"But Ken, darling, I thought we agreed. We're going to put a damper on spending until we get out of debt . . ."

"Cora, Cora, you don't understand. It's only a little camera, and a once-in-a-lifetime deal. Besides, you yourself said we need a camera! Think how nice it will be with Christmas and little Jen's birthday coming up."

This episode is but one in America's continuing drama of financial friction, martyrdom, and chaos. "Crediholics" like Ken and Cora, instead of using their earnings to pay off existing debts, keep adding new ones. This "debt on debt syndrome" produces, among other things, bankruptcy, ulcers, nervous breakdowns, and divorces.

Anymore everything from funeral expenses to court fines can be bought with credit cards. All the forces of our time conspire against the kind of money management that leads to financial freedom. Debt on debt as a way of life becomes more common all the time.

Ideally, money is a tool. It is a tool to be used in providing for life's essentials—food, shelter, and clothing. Money is to be enjoyed, put away for a rainy day, and shared with others. Yet ever since money was invented it has been misused. All too often it becomes a god, with unyielding powers over man. Instead of using money as a tool for happiness and healthful living, man has all too often become the tool of money.

People sometimes make money the center of their existence and become confused about life's real purpose. Earn more, have more, spend more. In the process family relationships are destroyed and covetousness becomes a way of life. Jesus warned, "Take heed, and beware of covetousness: for a man's life consisteth not in the abundance of the things which he possesseth" (Luke 12:15).

Take Fred and Fran Adams, for example. Like so many others, they confused the strain for material success with personal worth. In their solemn quest for the proper house, the right car, the correct clothes, the right crowd, their family life was destroyed. So busy were they, that they did not find the time to pass on to their children the proper ideals of living. There was never time to share with them simple joys and pleasures. In their pursuit of material things, their family life disintegrated. Faith and love of God became remote and far removed.

Before the misguided success ethic took hold of them, the Adamses lived a quiet, but serene, life. On Sundays they attended church together. Then, in 1962, they began their rung-by-rung advancement from their simple life style to one quite grand. With each rise in their standard of living, however, there was a compensating loss in the quality and serenity of their lives at home.

Let me explain that the Adamses were nice, normal people. Fred started out as a bank teller, then was promoted to assistant manager. They managed quite nicely on his single income. They had a secondhand car, a small, but comfortable, home, old furniture, and a frayed carpet. However, when Fred became assistant manager, their "old" things did not seem suitable to their new station in life. In the grip of a passion to "keep up" the Adamses purchased a new home in the heights. Still, their "things" (frayed rug and furniture, old Ford) did not fit in with the possessions held by their neighbors. So after a family conference they bought all new trimmings to go with their new house. Now their budget was pinched beyond endurance. So they concluded that Fran *must* go to work.

Their children, Jack and Susie, were enrolled in nursery school, and Fran started her career. At this time they decided through mutual agreement to drop their church affiliations, since Sunday was really the only day they would have to relax.

In 1970 Fred was again promoted, this time to bank manager. Shortly afterwards Fran was chosen to head the ad agency where she had begun as a secretary. The couple, invited to join the community's most exclusive country club, now spent almost every weekend with friends at the club.

Meanwhile, back home, Jack and Susie were not doing so well as their parents. Jack, a teenager by now, had dropped out of high school. Pot smoking was his major interest. And Susie, shy and unhappy, had become involved in psychotherapy. Her counselor spent numerous hours trying to find out why she was afraid to be alone.

In 1979 Fred was promoted to be his company's regional manager. Fran was given a trip abroad to repay her for years of dedicated service above and beyond the call of duty. Then quite ironically, at the peak of their worldly achievement, young Jack committed suicide. Later on that year, the Adamses were divorced.

The Adamses learned late that things do not replace caring, concerned parents. And success, they found out, is not what you do or what you earn—it is who you are.

Both Fred and Fran got caught in the "star system" of their jobs. So much so that their lives at work replaced their family life almost totally. Jack and Susie, along with their vows of marriage, were heaped upon the sacrificial flame of "success."

To avert similar tragedy in our own lives, we must realize *God owns everything.* We possess, but God retains the deed. We earn, but God gives the ability to earn. There is no such thing as a self-made man. For God is the creator of the universe, the imparter of all talents, the great comptroller in the sky, so to speak. As C.S. Lewis wrote, "God foots all our bills."

Thoreau had sound words for today's debt-ridden, status-stricken families. His greatest skill, he said, was to want very little. This shining revelation holds hope for today's materialistic culture. To tame one's desire for things is to achieve self-control. Simple virtues meant far more to Thoreau than luxury. "Many of the so-called comforts of life are not only not indispensible, but positive hindrances to the elevation of mankind," Thoreau staunchly maintained.

With the cost of living continually on the rise, we would do well to hear Thoreau out, to ponder his words. If we are sincere in our quest for financial freedom, we must be willing to sacrifice things for peace of mind. Vow today to stop adding debt to existing debt. If you are in the habit of charging small day-to-day expenditures because you don't have the cash, then stop that practice. Make a new rule, *If I don't have the money I won't buy.*

Tremendous financial bondage can be overcome one dollar at time. If you are in the habit of charging groceries, resolve now to pay cash. Limit yourself to a reasonable grocery allowance and stick to it.

Discuss prayerfully with your mate all the aspects of your financial lives. To reach an understanding is a great step toward financial maturity and freedom. Vow never to use money as a weapon against one another. Consider giving up your credit cards or curtailing the use of them. (Recently I handed my VISA card over to my husband, for I was making far too much use of it.) Eliminate selfishness. Be willing to go without in order to establish fiscal sanity.

Form a cooperative financial team with your spouse, and proclaim your goal—financial freedom. Together you stand; divided you fall. I remember, for example, when my husband and I were first married. I didn't make the transition from a wheeling-dealing single for many months. I would go to town, find something I felt was a bargain, and buy it, without consulting my husband. When he was not as thrilled as I with my new purchase, I felt he was being unreasonable. But I was wrong. Now, I realize that I was operating selfishly. If I had consulted him, we would have been growing as a team.

The most basic step you can take toward financial freedom is to establish a responsible debt limit. Agree that you will not let your total liabilities outweigh your total assets. This means the sum total of what you owe should not exceed the sum total of the things you own. In our money planning, Marvin and I make it a rule to not borrow more than we already have in ready cash in savings. Now that we are building a garage, for example, the loan we took out is equal to the amount we have in savings.

For little day-to-day purchases establish a list of needs in order of their priority. If, for example, dad needs new shoes, start saving for that item until you have the cash in hand. By sticking to your list of needed items impulsive purchasing will be stopped.

Being systematic about money will put a crimp in your style. But gradually you will grow into a new, more mature way of life.

Financial freedom, you must realize, does not mean being so rich that you can purchase every desire of your heart. Instead it means achieving self-control. When we grow up in terms of money, we will come to realize that financial freedom in the truest sense involves freedom from miserliness or underhandedness where money is concerned. It is to be concerned and caring about others, sometimes even to share God's gifts with others in need.

Involved too is our good health. A lengthy illness can put any family in financial bondage. It is wise, therefore, to have good health insurance. On the other hand, we must take steps to prevent illness from occurring. Face up to the fact that you are responsible in a very large way for your own well-being. Get exercise, proper food and food supplements.

If you are overweight, resolve to lose those pounds.

As you grow into financial responsibility you will marvel at all the benefits that flow your way. Being financially free results in having more time. Time for spouse and children. Time for sharing; more time to read, to think, to pray.

Freedom from economic bondage involves an exercise in practical Christian living. The Golden Rule is put into effect when we repay our debts as we would expect to be payed. It involves being truthful (paying when we promise to pay). Further it means we are to become responsible stewards of all that God has given. Grass and hedges are kept neatly trimmed; houseplants watered; broken windows replaced; squeaky hinges oiled. Even more important than things are our families. Neglect of those we love is not a part of a truly free style of life.

So move sure-footedly toward financial freedom, one step at a time, one dollar at a time. By practicing self-discipline, soon the burden of financial worry will be lifted, and you will glimpse freedom's light at the end of the tunnel.

In the next chapter we will explore more practical ways in which we can be good stewards of all that God has given.

8

Fix It Yourself—and Save!

As mentioned before, financial freedom involves being conscientious caretakers of things already owned. For possessions have a habit of breaking down. Faucets leak, knobs fall off, lamps conk out. If you've hired a plumber or an electrician or a painter lately, then you know how costly house calls by these experts can be. The purpose of this chapter is to eliminate as much as possible the need for such specialists, or when you must resort to them to help you to get your money's worth.

When my husband, Marvin, fell off our new garage roof where he was shingling this afternoon, he landed on his feet. I am not surprised. Marvin always lands on his feet. He is one of those gifted fellows who can do almost anything—skilled carpentry, welding, wiring, mechanics, clock repair.

Marvin is the handyman's handyman. Only trouble is he keeps most of his secrets to himself. He's uncommunicative when it comes to revealing details about how things work or how they are put together. Like so many other geniuses, he's impatient with those with only ordinary talents. Intricate construction and repair come so naturally to Marvin that it's difficult for him to tolerate unskilled fingers that fail to hang a curtain rod right.

Marvin is the legend of the do-it-yourselfer. Always he is up to his elbows in grease or cement or paint. One project done, another begun. His energy knows no bounds. He's constantly saying things like, "See that wall there, let's move it over there." Just once I wish he'd spend an afternoon in an easy chair!

Still, his almost boundless skills have saved us inestimable dollars. When my typewriter breaks down, I have only to wait for marvelous Marvin. When the toilet got clogged (all the way to the alley), he rented Roto-Rooter's outfit and performed the massive maneuver all by himself. Once we did call an electrician, but when he read the bill, he resolved to become our electrical troubleshooter, too.

Always my husband is either going in or coming out of a hardware store.

In a sense, Marvin reflects an attitude

inherent with Americans. Historically we have prided ourselves on our great abundance of initiative and self-reliance. Backyard geniuses are forever in rebellion against high prices, red tape, mechanization, and standardization.

Blessed is the home with a live-in Mr. Fix-It. For the modern American home is a virtual humming and clanking complex of hydraulic, electrical, and mechanical systems. To call a professional each time something goes haywire is to stretch one's budget way beyond limits.

A rule of thumb—before touching the dial of your telephone to call a repairman, check for the simple solution. A great number of machine failures result from nothing more than a loose plug, a blown fuse, or a broken cord. Once I called the Maytag man (that fellow on TV with nothing to do, remember?). I was very embarrassed, for all he did was reach inside the washer to jog my load of clothes. Upon closing the lid the machine whirled into action and has been performing faultlessly ever since.

I discovered my clothes drier will not work with the door slightly ajar. Sometimes the push button on my dishwasher must be jiggled before it goes into action. The other day when my oven wouldn't work, it turned out to be a simple matter, too. I had accidentally pushed the "timed" buttom while cleaning. After resetting it to "manual" it lighted up right away.

By watching my husband over the years I have learned a few important things about home repair. Before beginning work on any appliance he is certain to unplug it or shut off the electricity to the appropriate circuit, or to shut off the water.

Marvin is meticulous. He takes it easy and doesn't rush. He is also systematic. Before taking anything apart he has me hunt up the owner's manual. Then he reads the repair instructions carefully. Next he pinpoints the trouble by determining what the machine is still doing right. A course of action is then mapped out. With my help we gather necessary tools and lay them out before starting to work.

Before dismantling he sizes up the assembled picture. And as he takes anything apart he puts down each piece in the order in which it came out of the machine. Marvin is good, too, at recognizing his limits. More than once he has stopped to dial up a hot line to get further instructions from a manufacturer. (If you need help from a company, call toll free 800-555-1212 for information.)

Whenever Marvin fixes anything his attitude is calm and purposeful. He is both systematic and organized. Bending over a machine he will call for "needle-nose pliers" or "hacksaw" like a dedicated surgeon contemplating an open heart.

If your trouble turns out to be more serious than a jilted plug and resists the diagnostic skill of your repairman in residence, here's a word of advice. Before tinkering with any appliance be sure to look up your warrantee. If it is still in effect, you may render it void by your efforts to fix the appliance. If so, return the product to the company or retailer for their repair service.

The more you know about your machine or appliance the better prepared you will be to deal with a serviceman and avoid victimization. For this reason get in the habit of saving all manuals, sales slips, warranties, and bills from previous repair jobs. Marvin and I have a large envelope into which we stuff all those booklets that explain the workings of various appliances.

When dealing with a serviceman, come to terms about money before he starts to work. Otherwise you might wind up spending more for the repair job than a new appliance would cost. If you possibly can, get him to give an estimate in writing. And ask that he notify you immediately if the cost estimate should happen to go up. For your protection ask for all the replaced parts, and make sure he gives you an invoice listing all new parts and labor costs.

Deal fairly, but do keep your relationship businesslike, so that you will not feel reluctant to be firm in such matters.

Besides being a mechanical troubleshooter, Marvin has saved us money by insulating our house. After insulating, we found we were more comfortable both summer and winter. Even better, we were richer. The winter after he had insulated walls and ceilings our heat bill dropped 40 percent in spite of a hike in fuel prices. The value of your home is increased by insulation, too. Insulating is one of the home improvements that help to raise the value and increase the market potential if you should want to sell.

We used aluminum foil with inflammable spun fiber in our walls and ceilings. (This was possible because Marvin had torn out all the existing plaster and lathes.) By doing it ourselves the cost of the project was reduced by half. Tools needed included lawn shears (to cut the rolls of insulation) and a large staple gun.

Marvin's nearly expert knowledge of cars has saved money, too, over the years. Owning an automobile is a necessity, but keeping it repaired can become a nightmare if one is ignorant of its engine's internal workings. Americans pay out an estimated $29 billion a year to repair more than 110 million vehicles. Of this, roughly $10 billion is wasted on shoddy or overpriced repairs.

Car owners who do not have basic engine knowledge become sitting ducks for all the tricksters of the mechanic's trade. Often, for instance, an operator will sell a customer a new battery, when cleaning the terminals or adding water to the old one would do.

If you don't know about car engines, then learn. Go to your library and check out books. *Consumer Guide* publishes an illustrated *Car Tune-Up Guide* for $2.50. Subscribe to *Mechanix Illustrated.* If you can, take a mechanic's course. Home extension services sometimes offer lessons in engine repair for beginners.

Another big way we have saved money on upkeep is by do-it-yourself painting. When we bought our house in Lakeview, the paint job was almost twenty years old. A contractor gave us an estimate of almost $1500 to do the job. "We'll do it ourselves," we agreed.

One fall afternoon I began with brush and pail and ladder. It was one of those aluminum extension ladders, very heavy in fact. Luckily my daughter, Kirsten, was playing nearby, for when I tried to move it, the thing came tumbling down on me, entrapping me between its rungs. Cars came and went along our busy street, but none of the drivers seemed to notice I was having trouble. Finally Kirsten ran next door to get our neighbor, who lifted it away, saving me from its steely clutches.

Right and wrong ways there are to move ladders! When the ladder is fully raised, lean the upper end gently against the house. To move sideways tilt the upper end a few inches first, and then slide the bottom half over.

Painting a two-story house is slow work if your tools are paintbrush and roller. Investing in a compressor and spray gun was a smart thing, for after that Marvin finished the second coat in two days.

Invest in good paint, for 75 percent of the cost of a paint job is labor, and when it is your own backbreaking labor, long-lasting material becomes even more dear. We used Sears top-quality outdoor paint inside and out, because we both dislike painting. It paid off, for the outdoor paint inside held up for five years with hardly a nick or scratch.

It pays, too, to buy good tools, because you will use them for as long as you maintain a home. Before you start to paint prepare yourself by getting your painting gear together. Ladder, roller, brushes, and so on. A threaded extension makes painting broad areas almost easy. (This can be purchased at any hardware store. It is a long, broomlike handle that screws into the top of your roller.)

Take your time. Be especially patient when you get to those close places that must be touched up with a brush. Temporarily remove all doorknobs, bric-a-brac, light fixtures, and electrical switch plates. Remove grease stains on the wall with a detergent solution. If you don't, they will show through many paints. Scrape and brush away all scaling or powdery paint.

Don't be misled by one-coat paint. It works only if applied over walls or ceiling of about the same color and in good condition. New, unpainted surfaces—or badly discolored or dark ones—will generally require two or three coats. Some of the new water-base paints dry so quickly that it is feasible to apply two coats in the same day.

Devise a plan of action. Paint ceilings first. Dip the roller into the paint tray and apply in any pattern, crisscrossing for even spreading.

The secret of professional edging is tedious, yet fairly simple. Beginners often resort to masking tape or buy a number of not-too-satisfactory edging devices. Here's how the professional achieves those neat borders. Work freehand, letting your ceiling color extend down the wall a half inch or so. After it dries, take a tiny brush to mark a line of overlapping wall color all the way to where the wall joins the ceiling. If wall paint overlaps onto the ceiling it will not be too noticeable. And failure of the wall color to cover all the wall appears as a wavy line.

Allow the wall paint to extend onto the sides of door and window frames. When it dries, trace a line of woodwork color down the sides of the edge, being careful to stay away from the wall. This line will appear straight.

Painting, roofing, overhauling an engine—the handyman's work is never done.

When Marvin gets our garage finished, he plans to take out the fireplace upstairs and move it downstairs. Then he plans to build a redwood fence, and a patio, and to do some landscaping. While others spend their money on expensive trips, we plant ours right here in our own backyard!

9

You Can Be Beautiful

Do-it-yourself extends to almost every phase of our lives. From upkeep of our home and car to the personal realm of beauty. If you are like me, you seldom find your pocketbook flush enough for a trip to the beauty parlor. So aside from permanents and an occasional haircut, homespun beauty becomes a way of life.

Do you ever study those pages in the magazines with models who are so perfect they resemble mannequins? Carefully lined eyes, perfect figures—these models know all the latest tricks in makeup and how to get themselves together. By any standard they are striking, and by some even beautiful. Mentally I calculate the price tag attached to her up-to-the-minute look, her hair, the fashion, the coat. Even if I could afford it, *is it me!*

Outwardly so many of these gals are really gorgeous, but *inwardly!* Their eyes betray them. Inwardly for so many there appears to be a missing dimension in their lives. After a thorough search through the pages of one popular women's magazine I became more convinced than ever. In order to discover true beauty one must walk among Christians. For as Castiglione wrote some 500 years ago, "Beauty I believe comes from God, therefore there can be no beauty without goodness."

But is goodness enough? We all know thoroughly good women who are not quite beautiful. In spite of their lack, a sort of radiance does shine through, however. At times I cannot help thinking wishfully of some of them, if only she would spend a little time and effort she could be a knockout!

It really takes so little time. And we feel so much better when those night-torn locks are brushed into place, and when we add a dash of lipstick, a bit of moisturizer.

Cleanliness and careful grooming are the basis of all beauty. To shower each morning, to repair chipped nail polish, to thin grizzly brows, or to shave one's legs takes only a few minutes. And how much better we feel when we present to the world a self who is clean and cared for.

The late caustic critic Henry Louis Mencken described the beauty of most women as "pure illusion." In his unflattering estimation the vast majority of women possess "harsh curves and clumsily distributed masses." So defective in form, he thought, that a cuspidor or milk jug compared to the female body is an object of art and a thing of intelligent design.

Harsh though Mencken's assessment be, he spoke truth. For there are in fact very few natural beauties. George Masters, the beauty expert of the stars, writes, "There is no such thing as an ugly woman, only the lazies. Behind every great beauty there is a beauty maker." In Masters's judgment there is no such thing as a hopeless case, beautywise. In his book, *The Masters Way to Beauty*, he tells of one international beauty who has almost nothing to start with, no natural physical endowments. Her nose is too big. She has buck teeth and no chest at all. Her eyes are poppy and her hair is thin. But according to Masters, she has a real talent for pulling herself together, and the look she achieves is absolutely stunning.

There is hope then, no matter how little nature has given. Even on a small budget we can strive to be stylish and attractive by employing a little ingenuity. If you have priced cosmetics lately, you will be relieved that my recipe for beauty on a budget involves very little of the stuff you purchase over the cosmetic counter. A smidgen of lipstick, a dash of mascara, a touch of blusher, and a dab of moisturizing cream can convey the essence of facial glamour that will cause heads to turn.

Perhaps even more important than rubbing things on the surface is taking pride in our total selves. More than narcissistic self-centeredness, the pursuit of beauty can be a path to greater self-knowledge and worth as a human being.

If you are a witnessing Christian, then looking your best becomes a sort of duty. When you know you look your best, it enhances your outlook. The way you walk and talk, sit and stand, helps you become more assured and animated. Knowing that you look attractive makes you feel confident. And confidence itself is an attractive trait. By looking our best we place our best foot forward for Jesus.

"Life has loveliness to sell," the poet reminds us. Unfortunately, in a personal sense that loveliness does not spring up in full blossom accidentally. Even natural beauties must work at it. Have you noticed that natural beauties often fade the fastest? If you attend a class reunion, be sure to notice how the campus queen is holding up. Many girls who start out with peaches and cream complexions and perfect figures are especially prone to the lazies. They think they've got it made, and they fail to acquire good beauty habits. Ironically then, by the time they're thirty-five, they're outshone by the ugly ducklings who formerly envied them.

Genuine beauty, we know, is much more than a pretty face. For what we are, how we spend our time, the way we treat others, our inner convictions—all these are revealed on our faces. Believing in Jesus costs nothing, but His presence in our lives shows. Says Joyce Landorf, "No matter how a woman fixes her face or her hair or takes care of her outer looks, if she has not Christ, she will have no real beauty. She will be like a flower with no perfume, no fragrance, no essence to remember."

Serenity is vital to beauty, and it is bolstered by prayer. It costs absolutely nothing to pray. And prayer is a vital beauty treatment in itself. Time spent on one's hands and knees erases those unattractive worry lines. Confession of sin and forgiveness of others shows on our faces, too. Have you ever seen a woman with lovely features who was scarred by lines of hatred? Attitudes of unforgiveness are quickly etched into our skin. Also, the superior smirk and pursed lips of the judgmental are never pretty to look at.

Soul beauty, however, should not be taken for granted. A few of the Christian ladies who seem to be permanently at rest on the laurels of their salvation really should go to work on themselves. Some of them are so certain of their standing with God that they don't even bother with deodorant. Their attitude is "I am saved, and that's all that matters." If only they would take pride in themselves and their looks, how much better representatives of their faith they would be.

Still another aspect of looking good on a limited budget involves the things we eat. Actually it costs no more to buy foods which enhance one's health and face and figure than to stock up on junk items. Feeling well is vital to looking good.

A woman's posture, for example, is a dead giveaway of attitude and age. Rounded shoulders and sunken chest mark a woman old before her time. Such posture defects can be avoided by exercise and good diet, with plenty of vitamin E and minerals.

Beware of refined carbohydrates and salty foods. Fill up on garden items—carrots, celery, green pepper. To ensure adequate protein, eat cheese, eggs, liver, lean meat. Natural beauties invariably take vitamin supplements. They maintain that these are essential to looking good and feeling fine. "You are what you eat," says an adage, and that advice is very valuable in the discovery of beauty on limited means.

Many beauty defects are actually health defects. Take dull hair, dull eyes, or splitting nails, for instance. All of these can be corrected by eating right and getting proper sleep.

Still another aspect of beauty is your smile. No matter how perfect your face may be, if your teeth are bad or discolored, or if you have bad breath, you will not make a good impression. Brush your teeth after each meal or snack. End each meal with something from the garden, fresh and crunchy. If you feel your teeth are badly discolored, consider having your teeth crowned. Your dentist can explain how this works. Briefly, it consists of filing the tooth and replacing the portion with a perfect replica of the original.

To achieve that special glow, instead of applying gobs of makeup, exercise. Running, bicycling, and playing tennis bring out the natural color of your skin and lend a marvelous radiance that no amount of makeup can impart.

However, if you do feel the need for something special for your skin, don't use the drugstore cosmetics. Instead go into your pantry and discover beauty products smart women have been using for centuries.

Apples. These are good for oily skin. Use them as a toner. Slice a large apple into paper-thin pieces and lie down. Place the apple over your face. Leave on for 10 minutes and rinse with cool water.

Almond meal. Mix this with a tablespoon of water and knead into your face. Leave it on for 10 to 15 minutes and rinse.

Olive oil. This is a good hot oil treatment for your hair. Warm two tablespoonfuls in a pan of hot water. Massage it into your hair. Cover scalp with plastic bag, then with a hot, damp towel. Let set for 30 minutes and then shampoo.

Lemons are a good astringent and whitener for the skin. Some of the world's great beauties add milk and lemon juice to oatmeal to make a mash that cleanses and livens the skin.

Baker's yeast mixed with milk makes a refining treatment for oily, porous skin. Or cover pieces of *orange peel* with hot water. Let stand. This cooled liquid can be used as a face freshener.

Achievement of the kind of beauty that does not rub off on the pillowcase overnight does not need to cost a fortune. If you can, get some free pointers and techniques in one of those makeup studios.

Take stock of yourself. Decide which look is "right" for you, and then pursue it.

Start today. Even if you are not a natural beauty, you can achieve a perfectly stunning look, even if it be only an illusion. A friend who formerly despaired of ever having a date now receives wolf whistles. "If I can do it anybody can," she says. She started her gradual course in self-improvement two years ago, slimming from a size sixteen to a size six. She says she achieved her goal by prayer, push-ups, and pushing away from the table.

To care about the way we look benefits everyone—husbands, children, community, ourselves, and, yes, even God.

10

How to Feel Better

More abundant living calls for not only looking good, but feeling good as well. There seems to be, however, a national conspiracy against good health and fitness. I have discovered that it is not popular to be concerned about what one eats, or the way one cares for God's gift the body.

Recently my hometown paper ran a front-page obituary of a Joe Gallagher who lived to a ripe 107. In an interview before his death Joe attributed his longevity to "being mean" and "staying single," and of course he drank, smoked, and chewed. Gleefully my family called attention to the fact that old Joe had probably never taken a vitamin pill in his life, that he was living proof (though now dead) that all my talk about depleted foods was just so much malarky! I pointed out, however, in spite of an occasional Joe Gallagher, our American scene is far from healthy. It's true many Americans do survive to advanced ages, but how many of them enjoy robust health?

Look around. Consider the shape we are in. So many Americans (even Christian Americans) display the results of physical inactivity, gluttony, and apathy concerning the state of their well-being.

While many in this world suffer hunger, we in America face another problem. Hardly anyone goes hungry, yet proper nutrition is lacking. Paradoxically, many are overfed but at the same time undernourished.

As a result we are slipping. In 1949, for example, America was eleventh in life expectancy among the nations of the world. By 1969, however, the World Health Organization reported that we had dropped to thirty-seventh place. Every year cancer claims the lives of 300,000 Americans, heart disease even more.

In spite of these grim statistics, fitness and nutrition remain unpopular. To mention concern for health and the American diet often results in wearing a demeaning label, "health nut." Christians in particular seem to have an arrogant disregard for nutrition and the body. Perhaps this is an overreaction from the earliest days of Christianity when Roman pagans put so much emphasis on things physical, the body and its pleasures. Still, disregard for the human body is not scriptural. Biblical teaching correlates good diet with both health and religious life. Wrote the apostle Paul, "Whether therefore ye eat, or drink, or whatsoever ye do, do all to the glory of God" (1 Cor. 10:31).

Many of my Christian friends give lip service to 1 Corinthians 6:19-20, but not many really act on it. The majority put more emphasis on such things as mouth-feel, fun, sweetness, and jazzy flavor than they do on whole foods for properly nourished bodies.

I recall in the fourth or fifth grade when Miss Persimmon presented a lecture on nutrition during health class. In a half hour the precise Miss Persimmon delivered a lecture on the Basic Four that was to last many of her students a lifetime. Ever so briefly she touched on

    meat, fish, poultry
    fruits and vegetables
    dairy products
    bread and cereals

"Eat plenty from each group and be healthy," she said. But Miss Persimmon failed to convince us. For she did not anticipate the growing fondness for refined carbohydrates and other nutritionally depleted foods, almost to the exclusion of the fundamental four.

Clearly, the fueling and repair of the human body is a tremendous task. For each one of us is framed with 263 bones, 600 muscles, and 970 miles of blood vessels. There are 400 cups on the tongue for tasting; 20,000 hairs in the ears for fine tuning; 10 million nerves and nerve branches; 2500 sweat tubes to each square inch of skin; 600 million air cells to the lungs that inhale 2400 gallons of air daily. And a telephone system that relates to the brain instantly any taste, sight, touch, or smell. The heart beats 4200 times an hour and pumps 12 tons of blood daily.

It was only a few years ago that mom brought home from the grocery store proper foods for fueling and repair. But today, mom often opts for convenience items—instant potatoes, white minute rice, mass-produced white bread, canned soups, dehydrated meals from a box, hamburger helper, TV dinners. Foods today are pulverized, chemicalized, bleached, dyed, dehydrated, hydrolized, homogenized, emulsified, pasteurized, and gassed. On top of this, antinutrients abound. Physicians administer drugs which act as vitamin robbers. Our drinking water provides a regular flow of antivitamins, including chlorine, aluminum, sulphates, carbon, hydrated lime, and fluoride. Nutrition looms so vital today because most of us are simply not meeting the body's most basic needs.

Unfortunately many Christians follow the crowd in this area of their lives, instead of Holy Scripture. I attended, for example, a Bible study where a professing Christian invariably showed up with a six-pack of cola, which he would swill down in an hour. In spite of chronic kidney infection, he ignored his doctor's orders to give up his favorite beverage. We spent a lot of time praying for his condition, but without result. For things "not of the spirit" he exhibited an arrogant disregard.

Many Christians I know are living sub-Christian lives because they are not fully convinced that God created human bodies as well as human spirits. In fact, in many Christian circles I have found there is an almost total eclipse of the needs of the human body.

Is this scriptural? To me Christ's resurrection and ascension proves there is no legitimate explanation for this dichotomy. Genesis, the book of beginnings, presents an ecological system based on natural law, with man as the central catalyst. Man was instructed to propagate so as to share the earth's bounty. But it was also mankind's duty to nurture his planet and administer its resources according to law. Certainly His natural laws were included when God promised, "Take my words to heart, and the years of your life shall be multiplied" (Prov. 4:10, NEB).

Says Francis Schaeffer in *Pollution and the Death of Man* (Tyndale), "It is well to stress, then, that Christianity does not automatically have an answer; it has to be the right kind of Christianity. And Christianity that rests upon a dichotomy—some sort of platonic concept—simply does not have an answer to nature—and we must say with tears that much orthodoxy, much evangelical Christianity, is rooted in the 'upper story,' in heavenly things only, in 'saving the soul' and getting into heaven."

Contrast our modern way of life to childhood summers on my grandparents' farm. I remember the heady fragrance of apples ripening in the orchard, the taste of spring water as it bubbled up out of the ground. How cool and delicious it tasted with its faint flavor of rock and fern and pine. During long summer evenings I would turn the handle of the cream separator and help my grandmother as she churned butter and made fresh cottage cheese. Their reverently simple way of living made us feel at one with God and His universe.

Although unschooled in ecology or nutrition, my grandparents displayed reverence for their surroundings and the natural scheme of things in general. Their way of life was so close to God's loving earth that they did not have to weigh the questions that perplex modern men.

Off the farm in today's bustling world, it's a different story. Far removed are we from that ancient Garden of Eden, where food served as medicine. Concerning food as He created it, God said, "Behold, I have given you every herb bearing seed, which is upon the face of all the earth, and every tree, in the which is the fruit of a tree yielding seed; to you it shall be for meat" [Gen. 1:29].

Today, however, teenage diets (according to one survey) are only slightly better in terms of food value than those in the world's starvation belts. Six out of ten girls do not get enough protein, calcium, or iron. Future mothers ingest by the carload Coke, French fries, and candy bars. Diets almost totally devoid of nourishment are the norm for many of America's teenagers.

Yet, no warning is sounded.

A child dies of cancer, and Christians as well as non-Christians are swift to blame God. Would it not be more logical to indict a way of life that provides a steady diet of junk? Says Russell J. Thomsen, M.D., in *Medical Wisdom From the Bible* (Spire), "In the health laws given by God through Moses was the conditional aspect—obey and enjoy good health, disobey and suffer illness."

Many of my Christian friends, when illness strikes, say solemnly, "It's God's will." Thus, they remove from their own frail shoulders responsibility for looking after their own health or the health of loved ones. Not long ago I overheard a woman complain as we left our little church, "I guess it isn't God's will for my family to be well." (In less than a month they had payed out $21,000 in doctor and hospital bills.)

What should be the Christlike attitude concerning health and fitness? Scriptures tell us that Paul prayed for human bodies as well as spirits. And the record of Jesus' ministry clearly reveals that He was as concerned with ailing bodies as with broken spirits.

We must admit God does permit sickness. Sometimes He uses it to slow us down, or to instruct us in humility. Still, those who lay blame on God for a general decline in health will be hard pressed to find biblical references to back them up.

Laws of health are biblical. (Make a search of the Scriptures pertaining to health and well-being. You will discover many.) The Lord's natural laws apply universally to everyone, saint and sinner alike. And when fundamental laws are broken or abandoned (as they have been by many Christians today), then there is a price to pay.

Our heavenly Father provides abundantly for fitness and health. There are varieties of wholesome foods as described in early chapters of Holy Scripture. In this lovely world there is space aplenty for walking, cycling, jogging, swimming. Whose fault is it if we fail to take advantage of His abundant provisions?

In today's world, not just good cooks, but nutritionists are needed. It would behoove each of us to learn as much as possible, then, about vitamins and minerals, and nutrition in general, so that we might have proper guidelines in feeding our families. First, there is vitamin A. This nutrient plays a role in every function of the body. During illness and stress it is especially needed. Vitamin A is found in green and yellow vegetables, liver, eggs, and cheese. During flu and cold season I have found supplements of cod liver oil (a rich source of vitamin A) a great help in reducing ailments of this kind.

Important too are the B vitamins. Included in the B complex are thiamine, riboflavin, niacin, B-6, and B-12. These complex chemicals are necessary for nerves and fueling and repair. During illness, pregnancy, adolescence, and old age the B vitamins act as bolstering agents.

Another vital nutrient is vitamin E. It protects the developing fetus from miscarriage during the crucial early months of pregnancy. It subdues cancer cells, speeds healing, and prevents ulcers. The pain of angina is alleviated with this nutrient, and it regulates the consistency of the blood, guarding against strokes and heart attacks. One nutrient, it seems, could not accomplish so much, yet clinical tests show that vitamin E promises all these and more.

Another vitamin is C. Not long ago it made headlines and became the focus of controversy when Nobel Prize winner Dr. Linus Pauling advocated large dosages to ward off colds and flu. Some studies indicate it is effective against cancer when given in large doses. Vitamin C is so important because it is the prime ingredient of collagen (a glue-like substance that literally holds our bodies together). Sources of vitamin C are fresh fruits and berries.

A great variety of enzymes and minerals are needed, too. Most plentiful is calcium. Our skeletal system contains two to three pounds, and we constantly use it during the routine processes of metabolism.

(We covered the various trace minerals in a previous chapter.)

In brief we have touched upon the main elements of nutrition. Find out more. Go to your library and check out books on the subject. Frequent your health store. There you will find vast amounts of information concerning good health and nutrition.

Christians in particular must be concerned about nature and natural health. For our bodies are not really ours. They are on loan to us from our heavenly Father. Thus, proper upkeep becomes imperative.

For my family it has been a shaking up process. Instead of blindly following Betty Crocker, I now study nutrition and means of organic gardening. By trading spoon and apron for shovel and hoe, today I raise many of our own vegetables and berries in our garden

We are learning to savor raw milk (rich in natural enzymes) from a grade A dairy, and we find we really prefer yellow-yolked eggs from chickens who peck and claw for their supper.

Other Christians are coming to understand that without knowledge about fitness, being a good Christian is just too much of an effort. Energy is required to work for the Lord, to pray, to love God and one's neighbor, and to move mountains of unfaith. Outstanding health is worth bothering about because it sparks the Christian to be an effective testimony to the goodness of a loving God.

On the other hand, those Christians who have no interest in nature have much to suffer. For God is the author, the creator, the maker of natural laws. And whether the mass of men choose to abide by them or not, the physical laws of good health go on functioning. The laws are inexorable; they make no exception for race, creed, or color. And when the rules are routinely broken by Christians and heathens alike, then all the prayers in the world cannot alleviate the suffering of mankind.

So begin today. Reorganize. Realign your thinking and style of life to conform to God's natural laws. It's a new dawning, revolutionary for many. Through proper care I can become responsible in a large way for my own and my family's fitness.

11

God's Gift of
Natural Health

To be fit emotionally, physically, and spiritually is a big order. We can achieve this goal with God's help. Living more abundantly calls for self-reliance, less dependence on experts, and ways and down-to-earth means to preserve our selfhood and self-respect, while at the same time saving dollars. This can be achieved largely through the gift of common sense.

Scriptures tell us that we are fearfully and wonderfully made. Our bodies are one of nature's renewable resources, self-regulating, self-cleansing, and self-repairing. From time to time, however, the human body breaks down. "See a doctor" is usually the first response to sickness. The possibility of self-help in the realm of one's own physical body usually doesn't enter our minds.

Years ago, hot chicken soup and a feather bed restored many a fevered body to health again. Mustard plaster, along with granny's worried rites, served to make her family feel better—whether or not her simple prescriptions actually worked. Today, granny and her feather bed are of the past. And chicken soup (now that it comes in a can) has lost much of its curative powers.

Don't misunderstand. I am not saying we don't need doctors. For we do. Indeed, there are instances when a physician must be called and the sooner the better. I do contend, however, that in our super-sophistication many of us are in danger of being overmedicated. There are many times when more than anything we need a good dose of rest in the old four-poster, a measure of tender loving care, and a spoonful of granny's old-fashioned common sense.

Nutritional experts are finding many of the sicknesses we suffer are the result of vitamin deficiencies. The family doctor, trained to diagnose a problem in terms of a medical approach and to prescribe a drug or surgery for the problem's alleviation, usually does not advise the patient how he or she could have prevented the problem in the first place, and in many cases could have lessened some of the symptoms, through a proper diet and through proper living-patterns.

For example, a neighbor of mine found

relief from phlebitis, swollen blood vessels in her legs, through doses of vitamins E and C (with bioflavinoids). Her symptoms had their roots in a vitamin deficiency. Proper diet could have prevented the problem in the first place.

Members of the medical profession try their best to bandage up the problems we often make for ourselves through improper diet. Certainly we should not ignore the remedies provided by doctors. But a more economical approach to health is to avoid the need for medicine in the first place, by avoiding the sickness through proper diet.

Sometimes, in spite of granny's home concoctions and barrels of vitamin C, your cough keeps you awake much of the night. Expert advice is needed. In order to get the most for your money, sound advice is needed. Here are some hints to help you in utilizing God's gracious gift of discernment when meeting with your family doctor.

As consumers of modern medicine, all of us are in the same bind. We have no way of knowing if we are getting good counsel from the doctor, good drugs from the pharmacist, good technical performance from the surgeon. How do we adjudge the quality of the attention we receive? Is that operation really necessary? Why all those tests? That new drug, how safe is it? To keep on learning from experience becomes expensive and oftentimes painful. For the fact is we must rely on the doctor or supplier to tell us whether or not we have been well served. If by chance we are dissatisfied, we cannot return the service or have it repaired.

Difficult, too, is expressing the lack so many of us feel in relationships with the modern practitioner. Doctor-patient rapport is not what it used to be. Actually, very little communication goes on in most doctors' offices today. In hospitals, too, there is a void. Everyone is so hurried that patients often end up feeling no more important than a stick of furniture.

Survival in today's medical marketplace calls for a questioning attitude. Not long ago, my fourteen-year-old daughter injured her wrist playing basketball. After examining her, the doctor told us that surgery would be needed, but until that time, he told her to take *nine* aspirins daily.

"Nine aspirins—isn't that a lot?" I asked.

I sensed that he resented my questioning his authority. Needless to say, we didn't go back to that physician. Instead I took her to a chiropractor, who prescribed neck adjustments, massage, and heat therapy, and along with this she was to squeeze a sponge for fifteen minutes each day. Today her wrist is completely healed. Had we not "shopped around," our family would have become involved in expensive, needless surgery.

Overprescribing is not so isolated as we might hope. Consider offhand the vast array of prescription drugs our physicians ask us to swallow. An article in the *New York Times* estimated that more than one billion drug prescriptions are written in the United States each year. Right now you may be on some sort of medication. Take a look on your medicine shelf. If you are average, you've probably had one or more prescriptions filled in the last month. Americans consume 20,000 tons of aspirin, 225 tablets per person, each year. We take drugs to pep us up or slow us down. For headaches, backaches, tummy pains. We take sleeping pills to soothe us to sleep and wake-up pills to get us in gear for the day. Physics, tranquilizers, diuretics, blood pressure medicines, birth control pills, decongestants, antihistamines, antibiotics, anticoagulants, weight control drugs, hormones, anticonvulsants, and so on.

"Take as directed" is often the only message we get concerning a prescription. And there seems to be an unwritten rule that we dare not question the doctor about the little white slip he hands us as we trip meekly out the door. For that matter, most are far too nervous in the physician's mysterious presence to think of challenging his smiling, paternalistic authority.

What can a patient do?

First, discard the notion that medical experts are infallible. Doctors are made of flesh and blood just like you and me. A degree in medicine does not confirm any sort of divinity. Another wrong idea is that drugs are safe as long as prescribed by a licensed physician. There is no such thing as a 100 percent safe drug. Taken by a susceptible or allergic person—or in combination with other drugs, or in excess—any medication is potentially hazardous.

To survive financially in the medical marketplace means you should have adequate insurance, as much as you can afford. Since 1950, the cost of keeping a patient for one day in a community hospital has risen by 500 percent. Nobody expects to get sick, but it happens, and being ill is very expensive.

Seek a doctor worthy of your trust, one who is a skeptic himself. Someone who does not believe the ads published in his journals without questioning. Make certain, too, he is one who reads the prescription brochures that come along with the drugs he prescribes.

Survival may mean taking an active part in your treatment. Ask questions. Read up on your illness. Find out everything you can about the drugs prescribed for you. If you can, get a *Physician's Desk Reference.* It will explain all about the drugs you are supposed to take.

If you must check into a hospital, remember that a patient needs concerned family members or friends who will act in his/her best interest when he is too groggy or intimidated to speak up for himself.

Before meekly submitting to surgery seek out another opinion. Find out all you can about the details of your case. Prayerfully weigh risks against advantages. Ask the Holy Spirit for clear vision and sound discernment. Then, and only then, decide.

Natural health remedies do work.

To me it makes good sense to seek out every possibility in promoting health for ourselves and our loved ones. I find it worthwhile to subscribe to *Prevention* magazine, a journal for better health using nature's medicines. To order, write to Rodale Press, Inc., 33 East Minor Street, Emmaus, Pa. 18049.

12

How to Have Happy Teeth

To live more abundantly means living without painful cavities and tooth extractions. "Look, mom, no cavities" is wonderful news. On the other hand, bad news from the dentist can set one's budget back badly. Preventing dental decay through sound nutrition makes all kinds of sense in terms of preserving one's pocketbook as well as one's teeth.

Says Dr. Jerome Mittelman, D.D.S., "If true preventive dentistry were practiced, more than 25 million Americans would not slip their dentures into a glass at night, or 98 percent of the American people would not suffer tooth decay, and 75 percent would not have gum disease."

According to Dr. Mittelman, good oral health involves much more than routine brushing and flossing, or even checkups. The essence of good healthy teeth, he maintains, is a good healthy diet. This includes the elimination of most refined carbohydrates and the addition of certain food supplements, such as calcium, vitamin C, dessicated liver, magnesium, and vitamin E.

Dental Abstracts (May 1966) points out that the vast majority of dentists learn how to fill cavities, rather than how to prevent them. Modern dental technology focuses on patchwork and repair. Dental schools provide their students with superb technology. Yet, out of forty-four dental schools surveyed in the United States, only sixteen offered courses in nutrition.

This means preventive dentistry, at least from a nutritional standpoint, is pretty much a do-it-yourself project. From observation we know that there are in this world many "primitive" tribes where people do not suffer from the dental decay and malocclusions that we in the civilized nations have become resigned to. For instance, doctors and dentists of the Adventist medical group, Liga, on a recent visit to Upper Cannibal Valley in New Guinea, examined the mouths of hundreds of natives. Not one cavity was found, and no missing teeth. Nary a toothbrush was to be found in the village, and fluoridation of the public waters had not been introduced.

Yet these people enjoyed perfect dental

health. This phenomenal oral record is the apparent result of what the doctors termed a "diet devoid of refined sugar and flour." Diet in Cannibal Valley consists of fresh vegetables, which are eaten right out of the ground. A wide variety of fresh fruits are eaten, too. No pop or candy machines are to be found in school halls, and they have no access to a bakery. Truly, a dentist in Upper Cannibal Valley would be hard pressed for business.

Can we imitate these simple natives? Only by giving up some of our civilized habits. Start with the sugar bowl (you know already what to do with it). Instead of something sugary, end your meals with vegetables or fruit. Crisp and crunchy apples, carrots, celery—these are detergent foods that keep teeth clean and decay-free. Use whole wheat instead of white flour. Professor Earnest Hooton of Harvard says, "Let us cease pretending that toothbrushes and toothpaste are any more important than shoe brushes and shoe polish. It is store food that has given us store teeth."

Remember when shopping that just because you see a product widely advertised does not mean the product is the best. Take soft drinks. Several years ago Dr. Clive McCay did some studies involving human teeth and cola beverages. He found that teeth dissolve almost immediately after being dropped into this fizzy liquid. This does not hamper the advertisers, however, in touting their product as the "real thing."

Phony food pushers go to almost any means to lure you to their products. And their subtle mind control works, for I see kiddies even swilling the stuff down for breakfast.

Subtle lies pack a wallop when people are ignorant of the truth. Take the breakfast cereals. Those who are nutritionally wise know that fructose (natural sugar) and sucrose (refined sugar) are very different in chemical structure and in the way our bodies use them. This does not stop the advertisers from claiming that the natural sugar in an apple and the refined carbohydrate of their product are one and the same.

Sugar abstinence is not the sole strategy in defeating tooth decay. Vitamin supplements reduce the enamel's susceptibility to erosion. Two doctors (Emanuel Cheraskin and William Ringsdorf) advocate calcium, vitamin B-6, brewer's yeast, and vitamin C complex. These nutrients, they claim, are both prevention and cure for tooth and gum problems.

Similarly, America's epidemic of dental malocclusions, or "bad bites," also stem from poor diet. Says orthodontist Dr. Vernon A. Nord, "During my dental training I was told that many dental malocclusions and facial deformities were the result of heredity. Most modern civilized people are a mixture of many racial backgrounds, we were told. The crossbreeding, therefore, supposedly led to dento-facial irregularities."

Through independent studies of natives throughout the world, Dr. Nord has come to think, however, that malformations of the mouth are caused more by bad diet than by bad heredity. He observed that in tribe after tribe, when the aborigines accepted the white man's diet, the natives became prone to decay and malocclusions.

In Australia, the primitive people enjoyed good dental health in spite of the difficult circumstances of their lives. Near-nakedness in below-freezing temperature affected them very little when they ate their native diet of mostly raw foods. All the diseases of the white men, including decay and bad bites, became the natives' lot when they began to eat the white man's diet.

There are a growing number of dentists (and I am fortunate to go to one of them) who believe as I do that "the real thing," as far as sturdy teeth go, involves more than routine brushing or dental checkups. If we want strong, decay-resistant teeth, then we must be willing to pay the price.

We must learn to say no to such culprits as soft drinks, sweet rolls, and ice cream. Eat instead whole foods—crunchy ones—and fruits, nuts, meats, and cheese. Forget the false notion that vitamin supplements are drugs. For they are not. Supplementary vitamins simply supply missing nutritional elements that the Cannibal Valley natives are fortunate enough to get right out of the ground.

Give your best to diet, flossing, brushing—in that order. Your reward in the form of better dental health will follow as night after day.

13

Pray Those Pounds Away

Refined carbohydrates have produced not only a bumper crop of cavities in this country, but a number of other maladies, including overweight. According to the U.S. Department of Public Health, over 80 million Americans are more than 20 percent overweight, and as many as 75 percent of all adult Americans may be at least 10 pounds overweight.

Our best-selling nonfiction book lists invariably include one or more diet books. This reflects the American preoccupation with this dilemma. There's the high-protein diet, the alcohol lover's diet, the water diet, and then there's always the pills with the promise, and Ayds. If you're like millions of other Americans, you have tried to diet, but to no avail. Could it be that you have been neglecting a source of power?

I have always prayed. However, it has been my policy not to "bother" God with small, seemingly inconsequential problems. After all, since our heavenly Father is very, very busy with a world chock-full of serious sin, crime, and disaster, I reasoned that a person should not pester Him with problems that he or she might better handle all alone—like being overweight, for instance.

I tipped my scale nearly thirty pounds too far to my right as I carefully scrutinized those numbers each morning. It seemed no matter what I did, that ornery needle wouldn't budge more than a few notches to the left. I tried everything—exercising machines, spas, jogging (uphill, mind you) five miles in one stretch. Nothing ever worked. Not until I turned my petty pound problem over to the Lord.

When it comes to willpower, I am extremely frail. Constantly I am tempted by food—all kinds of food—cakes, candy, pies, sugary jello, salads, pickles (the sweeter the better). Yet I detested the consequences of my overeating. I hated the way my clothes fit, not being able to get into my swimsuit or to wear my wedding dress anymore.

I finally realized that overeating is a sin. Gluttony as a way of life is as debilitating as drinking. Whenever I see an obese person waddling and wheezing down the street, I am reminded that by overeating we desecrate

God's holy temple, our human bodies.

The first step in my recovery was admitting to myself and to the Lord that I was hung up on food. My very existence revolved around planning three daily meals and making trips to the grocery store. No sooner had I finished breakfast than I awaited lunch. "I am a 'foodaholic,' " I finally admitted.

I decided that first week to lose two pounds. I accomplished it easily. By setting small, achievable goals, I have not become discouraged. And my doctor tells me that a slow, steady weight loss is far better for my health than one that is too swift.

Now, instead of experimenting with those tantalizingly fattening recipes so popular in the women's magazines, I read books and articles on nutrition. I discovered to my amazement that my human machine requires fifteen vitamins, fourteen minerals, and ten amino acids every day to keep in running order. From these body requirements I must synthesize an estimated ten thousand different compounds essential to my continued existence. Because all of these nearly forty nutrients work together, an absence of any one might result in the underproduction of hundreds of compounds essential to my health.

I now substitute whole-wheat bread for white. Not only do I find it more satisfying, it is more nourishing, too. Another health food, yogurt, provides a maximum in nutrition with a minimum in calories. Regularly I substitute honey for sugar, and wheat germ for at least one cup of flour in pie crusts, cookies, and cakes for my family.

I have really changed my style! All those gooey sweets I had indulged in for so many years, according to the nutritional authorities, cause much ill health.

Dr. Carlos Mason, a biochemist, has charged that overconsumption of sugar contributes to mental illness, crime, education problems, family breakups, and suicide. "Sugar is a concentrated poison," he contends. His studies over a period of fifteen years have convinced him that millions of Americans suffer from hypoglycemia (low blood sugar)—the body's reaction to too many sweets.

Knowledge of this kind really helps me to resist those tantalizing foods that I used to fill up on every chance I got.

Eating right and staying in shape is serious business. Medical researchers have discovered that 50 percent of all cancer in surveyed male patients can be traced to a lifetime of poor nutrition. The United States Select Committee on Nutrition reported: "Our eating habits and the composition of our foods have changed radically. The threat is not beriberi, pellagra, or scurvy. Rather, we face the more subtle, but also more deadly, reality of millions of Americans loading their stomachs with food likely to make them obese, to give them high blood pressure, to induce heart disease, diabetes, and cancer. In short, to kill them."

It's quite a firm indictment for me, for my entire family. We must either shape up or lose—lose our very lives!

Reading the Bible helps, too. The Scriptures have many admonitions against overeating. Probably the most impressive text to me is 1 Corinthians 6:19-20. It reads, "Haven't you yet learned that your body is the home of the Holy Spirit God gave you, and that he lives within you? Your own body does not belong to you. For God has bought you with a great price. So use every part of your body to give glory back to God, because he owns it" (TLB).

I feel blessed to learn that hunger is not fatal. Today I regard hunger as my friend. After all, without going hungry at times I cannot hope to lose those unsightly bulges.

Now when hunger strikes, I praise the Lord.

Exercise helps too. Slowly but surely I am gaining on my stubborn fat by briskly massaging those trouble spots around my thighs and hips. I run up and down the stairs and do high kicks and sit-ups. In the evenings my husband (who is a fatty too) and I go for long walks.

Jean Mayer, recognized as America's leading nutritionist, claims that a major factor in reducing is "high motivation." Prayer serves well here. By keeping a constant prayer on my lips, my motivation stays high. "Lord, don't let me overeat today," I pray.

I take full responsibility for losing weight, only this time with the Lord's help. I am weak, but my Helper in dieting remains strong. The Lord is there whenever my willpower weakens; I may call upon Him any time, day or night.

In retrospect, my weight problem could not be called trivial at all. Being in shape is important for me, for my family, and for God. Sad but true, I stuffed myself to the gills with rich, unwholesome food. Too often I found myself so tired I couldn't get ready for church to worship or to take part in Christian service or fellowship.

As a result of prayerful dieting, I feel 100

percent better and far closer to the Lord. Many of my friends want to know, "What are you doing for yourself?" Revolutionary! I have been programmed since childhood to eat three meals a day, yet now I know that the world will not come to a halt if I miss lunch occasionally or eat only an apple or an orange.

I now make a point of preparing for my family those foods closest to nature. Many of my favorite dishes in the past were loaded with unnatural chemical preservatives and synthetic colorings and flavorings, stripped of vital, God-given nutrients, and replenished with artificial vitamins derived from laboratories.

As I approach my final goal, I am not only thinner but a better, more confident Christian. Always before without Christ, my desire for food would overcome my desire to lose weight. By putting my problem in perspective and engaging the strength of Jesus in my battle, I have gained the willpower that always before proved unequal to the task.

One day at a time, one pound at a time— dieting requires enormous patience and persistence. Even with the Lord's help, taking off pounds (and keeping them off) is hard. I realize full well that overeating will always be a temptation for me. Yet with God's help I feel certain that I will not retreat into my old sinful eating pattern.

Every morning as I survey my progress before my tactless full-length mirror, I pray, "Help me, Lord! I can't do it without You! Don't let me overeat today!"

14

How Sweet It Isn't

Even in biblical times the drive for sweets was a problem, for a Proverb says "It is not good to eat much honey" (25:27). Most of us realize that a great abundance of sugar is not good for us, yet taming one's sweet tooth is not easy. At our house the battle against the sugar bowl is a never ending one.

After my last tribute to the sugar industry (birthday party), I vowed, never again. It was a guilt trip for me, watching all those children stuff themselves to the gills with cake, frosting, pop, ice cream—all of which I had bought. For I know full well that our earthly bodies house the Holy Spirit, and that as a Christian mother it is my duty to be concerned with the well-being and upkeep of those earthly temples.

Man cannot live by sugar alone, yet many Americans seem determined to do so. In infancy we offer sugar in the form of glucose water. Later we give baby juices spiked with sugar, and then puddings, ice cream, jello, cake, and candy. Sugar has become America's best-selling staple. Americans ingest on the average two pounds per week, two cups per day, one hundred pounds per person in a year's time. Never in the history of the world has a race of men consumed so much refined white sugar.

Unsupervised, many children exclude more wholesome foods in favor of sugary ones. Says Dr. John Yudkin, British authority on diet and nutrition, "Children in civilized nations get 25 percent or more of their daily intake of calories in the form of refined sweets."

Much advertising is aimed at sweet-prone kids. It seeks to persuade everyone that sugar is really a wonderfully wholesome food. "Sugar isn't just good flavor, it's good food!" one such advertisement seductively suggests. "Do you have that little impulse to say 'no, no' whenever you see your little one enjoying something with sugar in it?" the advertiser asks. "Lots of mothers have this prejudice. But, in fact, sugar can often do kids quite a bit of good. For one thing, you may not need calories, but children certainly do. They run around so strenuously that they sometimes run their supply of body fuel just about out. And at the same

time that they're running around, their
bodies are growing. Which means that the
protein a kid takes in should be used for
growth, not for energy. Sugar puts in the
energy kids need in a form kids like. It not
only helps youngsters stoke up fast, but the
good natural sweetness gives them a sense
of satisfaction and well-being. So the sweet
little treat that perks them up is also good
psychology."

Should we take Madison Avenue's word
for it? Is sugar really the wholesome food its
makers would have us believe it is? Many
concerned voices are being added to the
chorus. In January 1976, citing several evils
purportedly related to sugar, the Senate
Select Committee on Nutrition and Human
Needs urged Americans to cut sugar consumption by 40 percent.

Still, it is so natural for us to love sweets.
And supposedly the things we like are good
for us, aren't they? Hungrily we look to
sweet things as a reward, and I know well-
meaning moms who discipline their youngsters by proffering or withholding sweets.
Teachers use them, too. This afternoon my
youngest, Kirsten, arrived from school with
a lollipop—a reward for perfect spelling.

After all, as those sugar ads tell us so

explicitly, sugar is a great source of quick energy. In truth, sugar does contain energy, but that's about it. Various authorities estimate that the human body needs more than forty nutrients daily, and sugar contributes but one. According to the *Harvard Medical School Health Letter* (December 1978), sugar represents a source of empty calories, whether it be in the form of sucrose (table sugar), brown sugar, honey, maple syrup, or corn sweeteners.

Much of the sugar we get is actually hidden in processed foods. Check the labels on the packages in your pantry and see how many list sugar as the first and main ingredient. Heinz tomato ketchup is 29 percent sugar; ice cream, 21 percent; Wishbone Russian salad dressing is 30 percent; Coffeemate is 65.4 percent; Ritz crackers, 11 percent.

Animal or man, appetites are perverted so that sugar is preferred. According to a *Reader's Digest* article (October 1977), when saccharine is injected into the womb, the fetus increases its swallowing. Given a choice, experimental rats will consistently consume sugar water in preference to a nutritious diet—to the point of severe malnutrition and death.

Children react similarly. Take breakfast. The first meal of the day should be an energizer, for the morning's menu affects us all day long. Invariably, however, kids choose a sweet cereal over a wholesome one.

The sugar in your diet robs your body of essential nutrients, medical experts say. It's not yet widely recognized, but according to Dr. W. Marshall Ringsdorf, sugar depletes vitamins and minerals in three ways. Says Ringsdorf, "First of all, sugar supplies nothing to the body—no proteins, vitamins or minerals. Secondly, it promotes malnutrition by replacing more nourishing foods. If you eat 150 pounds of sugar a year, you're going to knock off 150 pounds of something that's good for you.

"Thirdly, sugar creates an increased requirement for phosphorus, magnesium and most members of the vitamin B complex family. In the metabolism of sugar, these nutrients are required to burn it up. The sugar comes into the body empty, and these nutrients then have to be taken from elsewhere. Sugar consumption is also hard on your body's supply of calcium. After sugar is ingested into the human system calcium is excreted in the urine. Symptoms of this deficit nutrition are things like headaches, insomnia, fatigue and irritability."

Dr. Ringsdorf denounced the all-too-common American breakfast of coffee with sugar and a doughnut as "not just zero nutrition, but actually minus nutrition. With no nutrients coming the body is drained. It would be far better to have nothing or just a glass of water than that kind of breakfast."

Dr. Leonard Haimes, director of nutrition at the Cedars of Lebanon Hospital in Miami, agrees that excessive ingestion of sugar robs vitamins from the human system. Says Dr. Haimes, "These are the so-called empty calories. The body still has to deal with them and break them down, and since no vitamins are coming in with sugar the possibility of depletion is set up.

In agreement is Dr. Wilber D. Currier, a specialist in nutrition and metabolic diseases and former instructor at the University of Southern California College of Medicine. Says Dr. Currier, "Sugar intake serves to deplete vitamins. The B complex, vitamin C and the minerals are particularly adversely affected. Sugar is empty calories; it has no nutrition in it whatsoever. It's toxic and harmful in many, many ways."

Regress briefly back to the days of the cave man. These early people ate berries containing only tiny amounts of natural fructose. Still, they did not suffer a sugar deficiency. Modern man, like the cave man, has the capacity to manufacture glucose within the body from other types of food such as fish, meat, and vegetables. Human beings are born with an ability to convert certain proteins and complex carbohydrates into essential body sugar.

Says Dr. Alice Chase, "Sugar is used to excess in the United States. Desserts made with sugar are eaten at almost every meal. In homes where sugar is restricted children generally experience superior health."

My experience amplifies Dr. Chase's observation. Outbreaks of colds, strep throat, and flu frequently occur as the aftermath of special occasions where sugar is starred—Halloween, birthday parties, Christmas. Kirsten, for example, has linked cause to effect. She refuses to eat powdered sugar frosting, for she identifies this supersweet with a painful sore throat.

Instead of eating a nutritious after-school snack, many children head to the corner grocery for soda pop and a candy bar. Wise parents insist that children enjoy instead more wholesome sweets which present no danger to health. These include wedges of pineapple, oranges, apples, and bananas. Truly, it's a sad state of affairs when so many moms have been brainwashed by Saturday morning advertising.

We must realize *sugar is technology's product, not God's.* Consider the steps in processing it undergoes before reaching the table. First, beets are topped, washed, and diffused through water. Then the product is heated and reheated, adding calcium phosphate, phosphoric acid, and milk of lime. After this it is boiled some more in order to remove the molasses. During this process virtually all evidence of nutrition is boiled away. At last, in its shimmering whiteness, sugar represents the purest of foods, yet the most depleted.

This summer I canned peaches and pears without adding any sugar at all, and they are delicious. When baking reduce the amount of sugar. If a recipe calls for two cups, cut it down to one and a half. I guarantee that nobody will know the difference. Limit the number of teaspoons you allow your children to heap on their cereal. It's not possible to eliminate sugar entirely, but it is fairly easy to gradually cut down.

Going against ingrained habit is not easy, but I have found by using God's authority, rather than my own, it is easier. I say, "God's holy temple is too precious to stuff with junky sweets," and this carries more weight than, "Don't eat that, it's not good for you."

15

Our American Way
of Plenty

Our heavenly Father has given us so many wonderful things for our enjoyment. But often we abuse His natural pleasures and make of them a perversion; our lust for sweets is but one example. Scripture says, "I brought you into a plentiful country, to eat the fruit thereof and the goodness thereof; but when ye entered, ye defiled my land, and made mine heritage an abomination" (Jer. 2:7).

Walk into any supermarket and you see a bounteous display of the outcome of our system of free enterprise and free trade. Apples from Australia, oranges from Florida, Yakima pears, cucumbers from California. In the clothing department we find Pendleton skirts, sweaters and coats; sandals and shoes from Italy; shirts, sweaters, and slacks from Hong Kong, Mexico, and Japan. Look at our highways. Everywhere people coming and going in their motor homes, strapped with motorcycles and bicycles, trailing boats and smaller cars.

Freedom has meant for the American people an abundance greater than that enjoyed by any nation in the history of the world. Freedom to build, to produce, to create, to travel, to trade. Our American way of plenty, however, has been both a blessing and a bane.

Outwardly everyone seems prosperous and busy, but inwardly there seems to exist a sense of aloneness and alienation. In spite of surface bustle and our constant preoccupation with things and gadgets, there runs an undercurrent of sadness. Symptoms of this unspoken feeling are myriad. Suicides, divorces in ever greater number, drugs and drug dealing. All bespeak our hidden despair. Crime, child abuse, juvenile delinquency, abortions. Thoreau, I am certain, would adjudge these to be outward signs of inward desperation.

Both men and women have become disinclined to involve themselves in occupations other than getting and spending, or pursuing pleasure. In this way, unwittingly they deny their own humanity. Today, according to Justice Lewis F. Powell, Jr., we are being cut adrift from the humanizing authority which in the past shaped the character of our people.

Children are scuttled to the back burner, enrolled ever earlier in day care. Likewise oldsters, who formerly lent an atmosphere of restrained wisdom to American homelife, are shunted into nursing homes.

With little grounding in faith or philosophy, so many fail to understand the real source of their feelings of alienation and aloneness. In the short stretch between birth and death we do not take time to consider, "Who am I; where am I going?"

In March 1945, D. Elton Trueblood wrote in the *Reader's Digest,* "The most urgent problem of our time is the spiritual problem—and unless it is solved, civilization will fail." Today we find much the same problem, although Satan has added some jazzy new fuel to the fire.

As Laurence J. Peter wryly notes, "When people become prosperous, they also become preposterous." In our cities emblazened in neon lights are samples of preposterous depravity in the form of massage parlors, "adult" bookstores, porno flicks. On the newsstand *Playboy* and *Playgirl* tickle naughty fancies, instructing in ever more erotic detail the art of immorality. "If it feels good, do it," bumper stickers implore. The family that swings together clings together, they tell us.

We hear all the wrong voices today. In public schools children are given the biological facts of human reproduction, without equal time for moral guidelines. In history classes they learn about Nero, but nothing of his distinguished contemporary St. Paul. Likewise, on television (with a few praiseworthy exceptions) we find "family" shows, but with swinging singles as parents. Talk shows zoom in on the perverse and perverted, while overlooking traditional values.

In material terms we couldn't be more successful, yet that success has not been translated into the moral or spiritual realm. Our plenty has often invested in the lustful pursuit of ego and appetite. So many want larger professions and titles, but with fewer demands and responsibilities. The work ethic, the cornerstone of any vital society, is scorned by many who feel that society owes them a living.

Instead of gratitude for God's great abundance we hear voices raised in discontent. Take the National Women's Conference in Houston. There women from all over the United States gathered to air their grievances against the system which enabled them, at taxpayers' expense, to jet across the continent, stay in luxurious hotels, and eat in sumptuous restaurants.

Privileges like these, however, were taken entirely for granted. Not one whisper of gratitude was heard. Instead we got only whinings of their victimization. The refrain for increased abortion on demand, day care, homosexual rights, and equal rights was broadcast loud and clear.

As Butler D. Schaeffer commented, "These women seemed unaware that there are in such places as China, Africa, India, women who are employed in menial labor from dawn until dark; who live with hunger, death and disease; who huddle in mud huts with the animals upon whom their livelihood depends; and who have no realistic expectation of improving their lot in life."

Women like myself who take home responsibilities seriously were not represented in Houston that week. We were not asked to share our views about the vastness of the spiritual commitment involved in child raising, or to explain why we are grateful to a system that has given us so much and such a wondrous variety of options.

The voice of the Christian has perennially been that of one crying in the wilderness. And the wilderness of sin has become so stunningly enticing. Such a cute little imp seems the devil, luring mankind to sin in such harmless ways. Not adultery, but respite from the monotony of monogamy. Never a lie, but a small evasion of truth. Not drunk, but tipsy. Never perverted, sick pleasure, but alternative life styles.

In his book *The Status Seekers*, Vance Packard tells of a spirited Negro lady who ran a small, but proud, business in his community. In discussing a well-to-do family they both knew, she dismissed them, indicating they were "common." This, in spite of the fact that they were worth a quarter million dollars, hired a maid, and drove three luxurious cars. This lady had no use for them because she felt they were "shallow, crude, and pleasure-minded." As far as she could tell, they had also botched the job of giving their children decent standards to live by.

This lady saw human worth in personal qualities, not money or things.

Other Americans still cling to the old values. There are many, I know, who are ever eager to lend a helping hand. In their daily lives they fulfill their responsibilities to mankind as well as to the marketplace. They live quite literally close to the earth. It is folks like these who are at the root of our moral order. These few are the "remnant" of which Isaiah speaks. And through these scattered few, we can hang our hopes for a better tomorrow.

The essence of living more abundantly involves a reassessment of modern values, a new appreciation for some old ways. It calls for fostering those qualities of mind which bring the greatest contentment. An attitude of gratitude is one such quality.

16

The Joy of Appreciation

From my Monday morning kitchen window I see a cemetery of rusting trucks, battered, decaying Fords, fading Chevys, clunkers of every description. On the corner a garbage can overflows with litter; a dog howls and whimpers on the end of a chain. Looking around my small apartment, I see unmade beds, dishes on the table.

Truly not much to be thankful for, I surmise. With homesickness, I fall to my knees to make another plea. "Lord, you know how unhappy I am, how homesick. Lord, more than anything, I need, well . . . yes—a better attitude! Please, Father, give me a thankful heart!"

That was many years ago. And although my life's circumstances have changed, and I have come up in the world in terms of material goods, frequently I pray that prayer. I ask the Lord to let me see His purpose—even in adversity—to let me see His will shining through.

Later on that morning, dishes done, beds made, I wrapped myself up and strolled through my neighborhood. A slum by certain standards, yet there was beauty even there. A yellow-headed dandelion shot through the sidewalk crack to stand solitarily against the March wind; a tiny bird flittered into the sky; a dark-skinned woman emerged from her humble home to shake a dust mop. Using the mop handle to search out the faults in the sidewalk, she turned to move back inside. Then I realized, she is blind.

At least I could see. I could lift up my head to view the sky. Not everyone is so lucky.

How often do we let the circumstances of our lives dictate the degree of our happiness. How often we make our existence even more miserable by so doing. Corrie ten Boom tells in *The Hiding Place* that she overheard her sister, Betsy, in her prayers thanking the Lord for the fleas that infested their cell in a Nazi prison camp. Thanking the Lord for fleas, she thought, now wasn't that carrying the attitude of gratitude too far? What good could possibly come from fleas?

Ultimately the fleas did prove a blessing, however. For they provided a sanctuary from the prison guards. So distasteful were these pesty creatures that the Nazi supervisors failed to keep their rounds. Thus, the ten Boom sisters were given an opportunity to carry on an undisturbed ministry of prayer and Bible reading among their prisonmates.

A friend tells me of a time when her husband was out of work. Too proud to apply for unemployment or charity, they were down to their last can of corn in their cupboard. Still, even over that meager meal they joined hands in thanksgiving, offering their gratitude to their heavenly Father. In a few days her husband found work, and they had groceries again. That experience, she claims, taught her a lesson that many bounteous feasts failed to teach. That experience of real want made her forever grateful for the things, especially food, she now has.

So often when I crawl out of bed in the morning, I can see only the grayness of the dawn and my life in general. My outspoken bathroom mirror magnifies all my wrinkles. I see a pile of dirty laundry, unmade beds, a nasty array of dirty dishes, and an untidy bathroom.

Then, when at last the beds are made, dishes done, laundry folded and in the closets, bathroom sanitized—order reigns again in my world. I feel a sense of success and accomplishment.

"Thank you, Lord," I pray, "for giving me the will to do all the unpleasant things that I must do!"

"In every thing give thanks," the Scripture tells us (1 Thess. 5:18). And that covers a whole lot of territory. It is especially hard for me to thank the Lord for failure, for the hurtful humiliation that comes into my life. Still, I have learned the most from those circumstances that have brought me to my knees. Even illness—a bout with Bell's palsy and near-blindness—taught me to appreciate the difficulties of the blind and those who are paralyzed. Through mental illness I learned to rely on His "everlasting arms" and to thank Him for the gift of sanity. By suffering I have learned to share the hardships of others and how to be truly compassionate.

Do we ever praise the Lord enough for the mercies of this life? For health recovered after illness; for a near accident averted; for daily guidance through His Word. For the infinite variety of this earth, the seasons— spring, summer, fall, and winter. And then again, for the seasons of one's life; for death even, for its merciful deliverance from pain-wracked or worn-out bodies.

I am thankful. For God's many mercies large and small; for all His wondrous blessings. For cute, smiling babies who have grown up into delightful young adults. For a cool drink of water after a thirsty walk; a prayer answered; a prayer answer deferred; a bed to fall into after a weary day. A view of mountains and trees and flaming sunsets!

Thank you, Lord, for simple pleasures, for lovely intimations of your presence. An evening walk with my husband's strong hand holding mine, accompanied by the noisy splendor of honkers arrowing their way southward. Wind in my face; the sight of the last radiant fingers of the sun slowly slipping into darkness and night.

Thank you, Lord!

In the midst of every adversity I have been blessed with a thankful heart—and this gift is well worth subscribing for and renewing. It is one of the most important keys to more abundant living.

Thanks for Coming!

At last we have arrived. Our mental journey has taken us up and down many a winding trail. Only a few of God's gifts for abundant living have been touched upon. I am certain you can think of many, many more. I am well aware that some of the concepts presented here may be new to you, perhaps revolutionary. But please keep an open mind and give them a chance. Go back, reread, reconsider. I don't expect you to adopt into your life style immediately everything outlined here.

Growth is a slow process.

In truth, however, none of the ideas presented here are new. Many are just out of fashion. But living abundantly does not mean that we will always be in style. It means instead that we retain a willingness to ferret out eternal truths which do work when we apply them to our lives. And the reason they are effective is because (if we thoroughly search our Scriptures) they are part of the inspired Word of God.